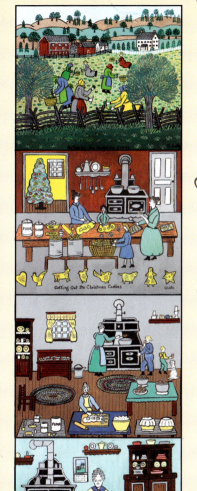

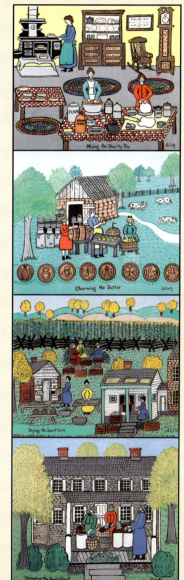

Folk Art and Foodways of the Pennsylvania Dutch

A collection of paintings, food lore, and seasonal recipes from the Allemaengel in Northern Berks County

Written by Jeff Dietrich and Lucetta Trexler Muth
Illustrations by Gladys Lutz

Published by the Albany Township Historical Society

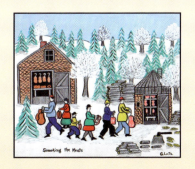

Folk Art and Foodways of the Pennsylvania Dutch
A collection of paintings, food lore, and seasonal recipes from the Allemaengel in Northern Berks County

Published by the Albany Township Historical Society
P.O. Box 95, Kempton, PA 19529
www.albanyths.org

Copyright © 2006
All rights reserved

No part of this publication may be reproduced, stored in a retrieval system, or transmitted,
in any form or by any means – electronic, mechanical, photocopying, recording,
or otherwise, without prior written permission from the publisher.

Printed in the United States of America by Jostens, Inc.

ISBN 0-9672433-4-3

Introduction

Albany Township is located in the northernmost corner of Berks County, Pennsylvania. The township was established in 1752. Early German settlers who arrived here were from an agrarian background and understood that after toiling to clear the wilderness they encountered, the rich loam of the forest floor, created over centuries, would provide fertile and sustainable farmland for generations to come. The Blue Mountain chain borders the township to the north with the "Pinnacle" being the highest peak in Albany Township and Berks County.

Many of the current residents of Albany Township were born and raised here, some on land passed down from their elders. Others come from distant cities, to live in a place mostly untouched by modern times. Nearby attractions include the Hawk Mountain Sanctuary, the Appalachian Trail, and the WK&S Steam Railroad. The serene beauty of the rolling hills, quiet valleys, flowing streams and still ponds compliment the 18th and 19th century fieldstone houses, homestead farms and small historic villages.

Among the missions of the Albany Township Historical Society is the strong desire to preserve and honor the traditions and places of our past. Educating the citizens of the present, particularly the youth, is perhaps our foremost goal.

In the summer of 2005, we were given the opportunity to advance our mission by recreating and reenacting the daily food preparations in a typical Pennsylvania Dutch "summer kitchen" at the Kutztown Folk Festival. The festival has been an attraction in Kutztown, Pennsylvania for over 50 years and each summer is attended by thousands of visitors from places near and far. Folks come to see the demonstrations of early Pennsylvania German folkways, admire and purchase examples of the traditional craft forms of the Dutch kept alive by contemporary artisans, and, perhaps most importantly, to "fress" or eat as much as they can of the traditional Pennsylvania Dutch fare available at the festival.

Summer kitchens on the farm generally contained a wood fueled cook stove or butchering stove, and a large wood fired bake oven. They were used in the summer months and into the fall to keep the excessive heat from cooking out of the main house. Often a smoke house was attached and the process of curing meats took place above the dome of the bake oven where the meats were hung on the rafters of the kitchen's roof.

Our experience at the festival, including the many questions from visitors about how to make the array of foods we demonstrated, prompted us to create this book. There are over one hundred recipes included here. Some of what you will find are examples of classic dishes made daily down on the farm. Other recipes are more contemporary, adapted by modern cooks using ingredients traditionally associated with Pennsylvania Dutch cookery.

The paintings that illustrate our book are the work of Gladys Lutz. Miss Lutz, now 97 years old, has graciously granted the

Albany Township Historical Society the permission to use her work here.

Gladys grew up on her father's farm in Lynnport, Pennsylvania, just a few short miles from Albany Township. As a young girl she took part in many of the earlier ways of life on the farm that those of us today who have banded together as a "historical society" strive to document and preserve. She completed her early education in the one-room schoolhouses of the area and eventually headed for Keystone State Normal School (now Kutztown University) where she earned her certificate to teach in the public schools. In 1928 she began her first teaching stint at the Greenawalt's one-room schoolhouse in New Tripoli, riding the "Berksie" train back and forth to her father's farm in Lynnport. Thirty-seven years later, she retired from the Parkland School District but, technically, she did not retire from teaching. Instead, she began documenting the rich traditions of the rural Pennsylvania Germans, from foodways to farming and the crafting of objects used everyday by the country folk. The results of these efforts are paintings, usually in series, that depict in a charming and naïve style, the daily lives and activities of our forebears. In addition to the visual imagery, Gladys prepared a short narrative, pecked out on a manual typewriter and attached to the back of each painting. These didactic pieces, which are presented here with her paintings, flesh out the images and provide more clearly historical documentation of the activities illustrated. At the Kutztown festival summer kitchen, visitors studied her paintings that adorned the front of the building and were apt to ask questions about what was depicted. Thankfully, if we were unsure at all about the details we could take the paintings down, read what Gladys wrote, and share the information with the festival visitors.

Because of her work, Gladys Lutz will never be fully retired. A great teacher never stops teaching.

Gladys Lutz, 97, March 22, 2006

Acknowledgments

We are grateful for the contributions of the following people who took part in building our book:

Lincoln Fajardo of Stone House Studios in Kempton, Pennsylvania, photographed Miss Lutz's paintings and provided us with production ready images.

Elaine Vardjan of Pennsylvania German Folk Art Papers in Reading, Pennsylvania, and her cousin, Dorothy Kalbach, designed the folk art graphics found throughout the book.

Gail Gottlund artfully arranged all of the components we provided and prepared our book for publication.

The good folk of Albany Township who support the mission of the Albany Township Historical Society with a tremendous energy dedicated to remembering the ways of our past and preserving them for future generations.

Contents

Because our book is organized seasonally, we have not listed specific recipes contained within each of the sections here. Instead, refer to the recipe index at the back of the book for contents arranged by food category.

SPRING

An introduction to spring with three spring menus...... Pg. 7

Here you will find ways to prepare spring specialties like dandelion, rhubarb and asparagus as well as other recipes to round out a spring meal.

Illustrations by Gladys Lutz:
Gathering the Dandelion Greens . . . . Pg. 8
Dyeing the Easter Eggs. . . . . Pg. 16
Baking the Bread . . . . Pg. 24

SUMMER

An introduction to summer and the menu for a Fourth of July Picnic. . . . . Pg. 27

Sweet corn, tomatoes and garden produce abound in summer. Gather friends and family and find the recipes here for a fresh tasting summer gathering.

Illustrations by Gladys Lutz:
Mixing the Shoo Fly Pies . . . . Pg. 36
Churning the Butter . . . . Pg. 40

AUTUMN

An introduction to autumn with a Thanksgiving menu. . Pg. 47

The busiest time of year on the farm, autumn recipes take full advantage of the bounty of the harvest.

Illustrations by Gladys Lutz:
Drying the Sweet Corn . . . . Pg. 48
Hunting Wild Turkeys. . . . . Pg. 52
Stomping the Sauerkraut. . . . . Pg. 56
Schnitzing and Cooking Apple Butter . . . . Pg. 64

WINTER

An introduction to winter with two soul-warming menus. . . . . Pg. 71

More than any other time of the year, the kitchen in winter is truly the heart of the home.

Illustrations by Gladys Lutz:
Smoking the Meats. . . . . Pg. 69
Serving the Pig Stomach . . . . Pg. 76
Frying the Fastnachts . . . . Pg. 80
Cutting Out the Christmas Cookies . . . . Pg. 84

Spring Spring

The earliest signs of spring in Albany Township seem to be those that involve food. As soon as the sun begins to warm the pastures and there is no evidence that anything is growing you will see brave souls out on their hands and knees digging dandelion greens.

Dandelion, the jagged edge plant that develops a yellow flower abhorred by gardeners, is highly prized as a culinary item by the Pennsylvania Dutch. The name dandelion comes from the French, dent de lion, or lion's tooth. For centuries this plant has been ingested in many ways as a spring tonic. In Northern Berks County the most popular way of eating dandelion is to wilt it in hot bacon dressing and serve it over potatoes. At its youngest, the plant has a bite similar to endive or sorrel. Once the flower has blossomed the greens are too bitter for most to tolerate. The flowers may be used for dandelion wine which is still made by many in the area.

After Easter and the formal start to spring, as peas, onions, spinach and lettuce are seeded; the rhubarb makes its presence known in the garden. Most every kitchen garden has several rhubarb plants. As the young rhubarb crowns begin to push forth it won't take but a week or two before the rhubarb stalks will be ready to harvest. The rhubarb will grow well into June providing plenty of opportunities for experimentation with the many recipes we have included in this book. As the weather warms up the stalks become pithy and are the victim of insects. When the weather grows cooler in late August and September the rhubarb may be harvested again.

Asparagus is the last harbinger of spring. Once the shoots of asparagus start to appear summer is not far behind. By Father's Day gardeners abandon their harvest of asparagus. While it is true that the spears start to toughen as the weather warms it is very likely that the growers are weary of keeping up with this persistent vegetable.

A CASUAL SUPPER
Fried Sausage or Ham
Boiled Potatoes
Dandelion Greens with Hot bacon Dressing
Buttermilk Custard Pie

SATURDAY NIGHT WITH FRIENDS
Pork Loin with Rhubarb and Dried Currant Chutney
Baked Asparagus in Lemon Sauce
Basic Mashed Potatoes
Rhubarb Pecan Upside Down Cake

EASTER DINNER
Baked Ham
Grated Horseradish
Scalloped Potatoes
Roasted Asparagus
Dutch Cole Slaw
Rhubarb Cinnamon Muffins
Coconut Sour Cream Cake
Coconut or Potato Candy Eggs

"Gathering the Dandelion Greens"

In the days before refrigeration, there were not many green vegetables for winter use. It was a custom in the Pennsylvania Dutchland that one had to eat something green on Green Thursday (Maundy Thursday), the day before Good Friday.

So, on that day or before on early spring days, women folk went to pastures and fields with baskets and knives to look for young dandelion plants before the blossoms appeared. Once the greens got large and began to flower, the leaves became too bitter for most tastes.

Many people thought of dandelion as a spring tonic, being just as necessary to use as sulphur and molasses. If one failed to eat something green on that day, the belief was he would get the itch or become lousy. The dandelion salad would help to keep fevers away all year, and, in fact its vitamins were good to use at that season.

The women dug up the young plants, took them home, cleaned and washed the leaves and put them into a salad bowl. A bacon dressing was made of bacon cut into tiny squares and fried until crisp. Then a mixture of sugar, salt, cornstarch or flour, beaten egg, vinegar, water or milk was added to the bacon and cooked to desired thickness. This dressing was poured warm on the dandelion greens, stirred well, and garnished with thin slices of hard-boiled eggs. It was usually eaten with boiled potatoes.

–Gladys Lutz

CREAMED CHICKEN

4 Tbsp. butter
1 small onion, chopped
1 rib of celery, sliced thin
2 Tbsp. flour
1 cup chicken stock
1/2 cup heavy cream
2 cups cooked chicken cut into pieces
1 cup cooked sliced carrots
Salt & pepper

Melt the butter in a medium saucepan. Add the onion and celery and cook over medium low heat to soften the vegetables. Sprinkle the vegetables with the flour and stir it in to the mixture to remove lumps. Add half of the stock and stir to incorporate. Add the remaining stock and cream and simmer for several minutes until it begins to thicken. Stir in the chicken and carrots and continue to simmer over medium heat until the chicken is warmed through. Serve over baking powder biscuits.

BAKING POWDER BISCUITS

2 cups flour
4 tsps. baking powder
2 Tbsps. butter
1 cup of milk or water
1 tsp. salt

Preheat the oven to 400 degrees. Sift the dry ingredients twice and cut in the butter with a fork or pastry blender. Gradually stir in the milk. The mix should be soft but not sticky. Add a small amount of flour if the dough is too sticky to handle. Transfer the dough to a well-floured board and pat it out lightly to one inch thickness. Cut the dough using a biscuit cutter or a sharp knife and transfer the biscuits to a buttered baking sheet. Brush the tops of the biscuits with a little milk and place the tray in the oven for approximately 20 minutes until nicely browned and baked through.

PORK TENDERLOIN WITH RHUBARB CURRANT CHUTNEY

2 lb. pork tenderloin
oil
salt and pepper

Rub meat with oil and sprinkle with salt and pepper. Grill on charcoal or gas grill until thermometer registers 150 degrees. Transfer to cutting board and let rest ten minutes. Slice into 1/2 inch pieces and serve with warm chutney. Serves six.

CHUTNEY

3/4 cup packed dark brown sugar
1/3 cup cider vinegar
2 Tbsp. water
1 Tbsp. peeled, minced fresh ginger
1 1/2 tsp. grated lemon peel
1 cinnamon stick
2 cups rhubarb cut into 1/2 inch pieces
1/2 cup dried currants

Bring first six ingredients to a boil until sugar dissolves. Reduce heat and simmer five minutes. Add rhubarb and currants and bring to a boil again. Reduce heat and simmer until rhubarb is tender.

DOUBLE BOILER SCRAMBLED EGGS

12 large eggs
1/2 cup milk
3/4 tsp. salt
1/4 tsp. pepper
3 Tbsp. butter
2 Tbsp. chopped chives

Break eggs into medium bowl. Add milk and salt and pepper. Melt butter in double boiler over gently boiling water. Add eggs and cover. Stir occasionally until eggs thicken. Remove from heat and stir until eggs set. Garnish with chives. Serves 6.

CREAMED SPINACH

1 10 oz. package frozen chopped spinach
2 Tbsp. butter
1 1/2 Tbsp. flour
1/2 cup heavy cream
1/4 tsp. salt
Dash of cayenne pepper, salt and nutmeg

Cook spinach following directions on package. Drain and squeeze out excess liquid. Melt butter in a saucepan, add flour and cream and whisk until thickened. Add spinach and seasonings. Cook for 2-4 minutes, stirring often.

BAKED ASPARAGUS WITH LEMON SAUCE

   1 lemon
   1/2 cup vegetable or chicken stock
   1 Tbsp. olive oil
   1/8 tsp. salt and pepper
   1 lb. asparagus, cleaned but not cut

Preheat the oven to 350 degrees. Into a small bowl, finely grate the lemon and add the squeezed juice. Add the stock, oil, salt and pepper and whisk to combine thoroughly.

In a shallow baking dish arrange the asparagus with all the spears facing the same way. Pour the lemon mixture over the spears to coat. Tightly cover the dish with aluminum foil and bake 20-25 minutes until the asparagus are tender. Serves four.

ROASTED ASPARAGUS

Roasting asparagus produces a sweet nutty flavor not usually achieved in steaming or cooking in water.

   1 generous pound of fresh asparagus
   1 or 2 Tbsp. olive oil or melted butter
   salt and pepper to taste

Preheat the oven to 450 degrees. Trim the cut ends of the fresh asparagus and rinse clean under cold water. Pat dry. Toss the asparagus in the oil or butter and sprinkle with salt and pepper to taste. Arrange the asparagus on a metal baking sheet and roast in the preheated oven for 10 to 12 minutes.

GRATED HORSERADISH

Peel and cut horseradish root into two to three inch pieces. Place in blender with white vinegar and process. You may need to add more vinegar to finely grate the horseradish.

Be very careful opening the lid of the blender as the fumes are quite potent and can burn your eyes. When the horseradish is of the desired consistency it can be placed in jars and refrigerated for many weeks until the strength slowly declines. Serve with meats or use in recipes calling for horseradish.

HARVARD BEETS

   1/3 cup sugar
   1 Tbsp. cornstarch
   1 tsp. salt
   1/4 cup vinegar
   1/4 cup water
   3 cups cooked beets, sliced or diced
   2 Tbsps. butter

Combine the sugar, cornstarch, and salt. Add the vinegar and water and stir the mixture until smooth. Bring the mixture to a boil and cook for 5 minutes. Remove from the heat and add the chopped beets. Allow the beets to stand in the hot mixture for about 30 minutes to absorb the flavors.

Reheat just before serving and stir in butter. 6 servings

CREAMY DANDELION DRESSING

Fry some ham slices in a bit of butter to brown them. Keep them warm and prepare the dressing in the same pan to capitalize on the flavors of the ham.

One nice bunch of dandelion
4 slices thick bacon
¼ cup butter
½ cup cream
2 large eggs
1 tsp. salt
Fresh ground pepper to taste
1 Tbsp. sugar
4 Tbsp. vinegar
A bowl of boiled, buttered new potatoes - hot

Carefully wash and prepare the dandelion, cutting off tough root ends. Spin dry or pat with a cloth to remove water. Set aside in a bowl.

Chop the bacon into small pieces and fry until crisp. Drain and sprinkle over the dandelion.

Put the butter and cream into a skillet and melt over low heat.

Beat the eggs and add salt, pepper, sugar and vinegar. Stir into the warming cream mixture and increase the heat. Continue cooking until the dressing begins to thicken and immediately pour it over the dandelion. Toss the dressing into the dandelion to wilt the greens and spoon the mixture over the new potatoes to serve.

HOT BACON DRESSING

The trick to this dressing is to keep tasting and adding sugar and vinegar until it suits your individual taste. It can easily be doubled.

3-4 slices bacon
1 egg
3 Tbsp. sugar
1½ Tbsp. flour
3 Tbsp. cider vinegar
1 cup water
¼ tsp. dry mustard

Cut bacon into small pieces and cook in a frying pan until crisp reserving grease. Beat the egg in a two cup measure and add the vinegar and water. Sprinkle the flour and dry mustard over the bacon and mix well. Slowly add the liquid mixture and cook, stirring until mixture thickens. Serve hot over garden lettuce or other greens. Some like dandelion or similar greens wilted in the hot dressing.

PICKLED RED BEET EGGS

It is said that Pennsylvania soldiers introduced red beet eggs to the world. Mothers sent jars of the ruby colored eggs along with their sons when they left home.

2 cans cooked young red beets with juice
½ cup brown sugar
1 cup vinegar
1 cup cold water
3 small pieces cinnamon stick
4 whole cloves
6 hard boiled eggs, shells removed

In a saucepan, gently cook the beets in their juice with the rest of the ingredients – except the eggs – for about 10 to 15 minutes. Let the beets steep in this mixture for several days, refrigerated. Remove the beets and put the liquid in a jar large enough to hold it and the eggs. Add the eggs and refrigerate for at least 2 days. Serve cold.

On January 11, 1770, Benjamin Franklin, while representing the American colonies as an ambassador in London, sent a crate of rhubarb to his friend and noted botanist, John Bartram. The plant, native to central Asia, had been introduced in Europe by traders. The rhubarb Franklin sent to Philadelphia had come to London from Siberia. Rhubarb first appeared in American seed catalogues in 1829, and soon became a popular ingredient in pies. The Pennsylvania Germans often refer to rhubarb as the "pie plant."

RHUBARB CUSTARD PIE
CRUST

1 1/2 cup flour
2 Tbsp. light brown sugar
1 tsp. ground cinnamon
1 Tbsp. orange zest
pinch of salt
6 Tbsp. butter
3 Tbsp. margarine
2-3 Tbsp. water

Place dry ingredients in the bowl of a food processor and pulse to combine. Add butter and margarine, pulse again. Add enough water for dough to come together. Form into ball and refrigerate. When chilled roll out and place in nine inch pie pan.

FILLING

5 cups diced rhubarb
1 1/2 cup sugar
2 eggs
1 cup sour cream
3 Tbsp. tapioca
pinch of salt
1/2 tsp. almond extract

Beat eggs, add sour cream and other ingredients. Place filling in crust-lined pan. Bake at 425 degrees for 15 minutes.

TOPPING

1/2 cup brown sugar
1 tsp. cinnamon
1/3 cup flour
1/2 cup oatmeal
4 Tbsp. softened butter
pinch of salt

Mix together and sprinkle over partially baked pie. Continue baking at 350 degrees until top is brown, about 45 minutes.

STEWED RHUBARB

3 cups rhubarb cut into 1/2 inch pieces
2/3 cup sugar
2 Tbsp. water

Simmer gently in a saucepan over medium low heat until rhubarb is tender and sugar is dissolved. Remove rhubarb and raise the heat to continue simmering liquid. Reduce to 1/2 cup. Cool the reduced liquid and return the cooked rhubarb to the pot.

"Dyeing the Easter Eggs"

The traditional way to color Easter eggs in the Pa. Dutch country was to boil them in onion skins. The housewife saved the onion shells all winter long. The shells, eggs, and water were brought to a boil and were boiled in a black pot. A color ranging from pale yellow to a deep reddish-brown was produced, depending on the quantity of shells and the length of time the eggs were exposed to the liquid.

To color eggs with an original design, an old time method was to trace figures on the shells of raw eggs with a bit of hard tallow candle, then put them in the boiling water. The parts marked with tallow resisted the dye and remained white.

Sometimes, the eggs were boiled and dyed first, then decorated by scratching a design on the eggs with a sharp knife, stylus, or other pointed instrument through the dyed egg to the natural color. These were called scratch-carved eggs.

Commercial dyes were not used because many of them contained toxic ingredients. The Dutch were afraid that if the shell was cracked and the child ate the egg, there might be a danger of being poisoned.

–Gladys Lutz

SIMPLE RHUBARB CUSTARD PIE
Frances Wright Trexler

The rhubarb cannot be cut too finely for this delicious egg custard.

- 3 cups very finely cut rhubarb
- 2 cups sugar
- 2 heaping Tbsp. flour
- 4 eggs

Mix the sugar with the rhubarb until sugar dissolves. Add flour and mix again.

Beat eggs until frothy and add to rhubarb mixture. Turn into nine inch unbaked crust and bake at 350 degrees for 45-60 minutes.

RHUBARB APPLESAUCE

- 4 cups fresh rhubarb cut into 1/2 inch pieces
- 2 medium apples, peeled, cored and chopped
- 1 cup water
- 2 Tbsp. sugar or Splenda
- 2 Tbsp. butter
- 1 tsp. vanilla

In a medium saucepan mix rhubarb, apples, sugar and 1 cup water. Cook over moderate heat, stirring occasionally until rhubarb and apples are broken down and soft. Remove from heat, stir in butter and vanilla. Serve cold or at room temperature.

RHUBARB PECAN UPSIDE-DOWN CAKE

CARAMEL

- 1/2 stick butter
- 1/2 cup lightly packed dark brown sugar
- 1 Tbsp. rum or bourbon (optional)
- 2 Tbsps. chopped pecans
- 6 stalks fresh rhubarb, trimmed and sliced 1/4 inch thick

Melt the butter in an 11 or 12-inch cast iron skillet. Add the brown sugar and the rum or bourbon and continue cooking until the sugar dissolves and the caramel is bubbly. Remove from the heat and sprinkle the caramel in the skillet with the chopped nuts. Arrange the sliced rhubarb on top of this. Set aside while you prepare the cake batter.

CAKE

- 1 2/3 cup all purpose flour
- 2 tsp. baking powder
- 1 tsp. salt
- 1/4 tsp. nutmeg
- 1 cup sour cream
- 1 stick butter at room temperature
- 1 cup granulated sugar
- 2 large eggs at room temperature
- 2 tsp. vanilla

Combine the dry ingredients in a bowl and stir. In the bowl of a mixer, cream the butter and sugar well. You want this light and fluffy – don't rush it. Beat in the eggs, one at a time. Carefully fold in the dry ingredients alternately with the sour cream – 3 additions of dry, 2 additions of sour cream. You will end up with a thick batter.

Spoon the batter over the caramel and rhubarb in the skillet and bake in the preheated oven for 45 to 50 minutes or until a toothpick inserted in the center of the cake comes out clean. Remove from the oven and place a large platter over the skillet. Carefully invert the cake onto the platter. If some of the fruit sticks, carefully scrape it out of the pan and smooth onto the top of the cake. Delicious served warm with whipped cream.

HARRIET'S RHUBARB PIE

3 cups rhubarb
2 Tbsp. cornstarch
1 1/2 cup sugar
1 egg, slightly beaten

Preheat the oven to 425 degrees.
Sprinkle rhubarb with cornstarch. Add egg and sugar. Mix well. Turn into a well-chilled pie shell and bake in a preheated 425 degree oven for 30 minutes. Reduce the temperature to 325 degrees for 15-20 minutes more.

RHUBARB CRISP

8 cups diced rhubarb
1 cup sugar
1 Tbsp. grated orange zest
2 Tbsp. cornstarch
1/3 cup Cointreau or other orange liqueur
1 1/2 cups butter, cold and cut into pieces
2 cups flour
1 cup oatmeal
3/4 cup brown sugar
1 Tbsp. cinnamon
3/4 cup slivered almonds
pinch of salt
1 egg

Toss rhubarb with sugar and orange zest in 3 quart baking dish. Dissolve cornstarch in Cointreau, add to rhubarb and blend. Preheat oven to 350 degrees. Combine other ingredients except the egg to make crumb topping. Add the egg to bind the ingredients.

Spread evenly over rhubarb. Bake until top is brown and rhubarb is bubbly, about 50 minutes. Serve warm with vanilla ice cream.

RHUBARB CAKE

A versatile cake that can be served as a coffee cake or for dessert.

CAKE

- 2/3 cups shortening
- 2 cups sugar
- 2 eggs
- 3 cups flour
- 1 tsp. cinnamon
- 2 tsp. baking soda
- 2 tsp. vanilla
- 4 cups rhubarb cut into 1/4 inch pieces

Cream shortening and sugar. Add eggs. Mix in dry ingredients and stir in rhubarb.

Mixture will be dough like. Spread in the bottom of a 9x13 inch pan.

TOPPING

- 1 cup brown sugar
- 4 Tbsp. butter, melted
- 4 Tbsp. flour
- 1 cup chopped walnuts

Mix together topping ingredients and spread on the unbaked cake batter. Bake at 350 degrees for 50-60 minutes.

CINNAMON RHUBARB MUFFINS

- 1 1/2 cups flour
- 1/2 cup plus 1 Tbsp. sugar, divided
- 2 tsp. baking powder
- 1 1/4 tsp. ground cinnamon, divided
- 1/4 tsp. salt
- 1 egg, beaten
- 2/3 cup buttermilk
- 1/4 cup butter or margarine, melted
- 1/2 cup rhubarb, finely diced
- 1/4 cup peach preserves

In a bowl combine flour, 1/2 cup sugar, baking powder, 1 tsp. cinnamon and salt.

Combine egg, buttermilk and butter and stir into dry ingredients just until moistened.

Spoon 1 Tbsp. of batter into nine greased or paper-lined muffin cups. Combine rhubarb and preserves and place 1 Tbsp. in the center of each cup. Do not spread. Top with remaining batter. Combine remaining sugar and cinnamon; sprinkle over batter. Bake at 400 degrees for 20 minutes or until top of muffin springs back when slightly touched in the center.

Spring

RHUBARB TORTE
Lucy Muth

This recipe is dearly loved by my family and has turned many into confirmed rhubarb lovers.

CRUST

1 cup flour
5 Tbsp. confectioner's sugar
1/2 cup softened butter

Combine and press into a tart pan or a 9x11 inch baking pan. Bake at 350 degrees for 15 minutes or until just starting to brown.

FILLING

1 1/2 cup sugar
1/4 cup flour
3/4 tsp. baking powder
1/4 tsp. salt
2 cups finely chopped rhubarb
1/4 cup finely chopped walnuts
4 eggs beaten until frothy
1/2 tsp. vanilla or almond extract

While crust is baking combine the sugar, flour, baking powder and salt together with the rhubarb. Add the beaten eggs, vanilla and walnuts. Mix well and spread over the baked crust. Bake 40 more minutes.

RHUBARB BARS
Jan Shrawder

3 cups raw rhubarb cut into one inch pieces
1 1/4 cups sugar
2 Tbsp. Corn starch
1/4 cup water

Cook in saucepan, stirring frequently, until thick.

1 tsp. vanilla
1 1/2 cups oatmeal
1 1/2 cups flour
3/4 cup brown sugar
1/2 tsp. baking soda
1 cup butter
1/2 cup chopped walnuts

Mix together until crumbly and pack 3/4 cups of this mixture into a 9x13 inch ungreased baking pan. Pour rhubarb mixture over crust and sprinkle with remaining crumbs. Bake at 375 degrees until brown and bubbly, about one hour. This will brown easily. You may need to cover it with a lose piece of foil if it darkens too quickly. Cool and cut into bars.

BASIC PIE CRUST

This recipe makes 2 single 8 to 10 inch piecrusts or 1 double crust pie. The technique described here involves a food processor but this can be made just as well using a hand held pastry blender and traditional ways.

2 1/2 **cups flour**
1 **tsp. salt**
1 **tsp. sugar**
2 **sticks of cold, unsalted butter cut into small pieces**
1/4 **to** 1/2 **cup ice water**

Put the flour salt and sugar in the bowl of a food processor fitted with a steel blade and pulse to combine. Distribute the cubed butter over the flour and pulse again for about 10 seconds until the mixture resembles coarse meal. With the motor running, drizzle ice water through the feed tube drop by drop, until the dough just begins to hold together. This should not be wet or sticky. Turn the dough out onto a large piece of plastic wrap and gather it together into a ball. Divide the ball in half and place one of the halves on another piece of plastic wrap. Gather the wrap around the dough balls and press to flatten into round discs. Refrigerate and chill for at least 1 hour before rolling out crusts. The dough may also be frozen for future use.

BASIC PIE CRUMBS

3/4 **cup all purpose flour**
3 **Tbsps. butter at room temperature**
1/4 **cup light brown**
1/4 **cup granulated sugar**
pinch of salt

Cut the ingredients together with a pastry blender or rub the mixture through your fingers until a fine crumb results. Sprinkle evenly over the top of the pie filling before baking.

BUTTERMILK CUSTARD

2 **cups sugar**
4 **Tbsps. flour**
4 **eggs**
4 **Tbsps. melted butter**
2 **tsp. vanilla**
1 **cup buttermilk**

Preheat the oven to 350 degrees.
Mix the sugar, flour, eggs, and butter in a bowl. Don't skimp on the mixing – make it nice and fluffy. Stir in the vanilla and the buttermilk.
Pour into a well-chilled prepared pie shell and bake in the lower third of the oven for about 45 minutes until the center is just set.
Cool and serve chilled.

COCONUT SOUR CREAM CAKE

A wonderful cake for Easter dinner.

¾ cup butter
1½ cups sugar
¾ cup sour cream
1 tsp. vanilla
4 egg whites
3 cups flour
¾ tsp. baking soda
2 tsp. baking powder
¾ tsp. salt
1¼ cup milk
1 cup coconut

Cream butter and sugar, add sour cream and vanilla. Sift together dry ingredients and add alternately with the milk. Add coconut. Beat egg whites into stiff peaks and fold into batter. Pour into three nine inch greased and floured cake pans. Bake at 350 degrees for 30-35 minutes. Cool on racks and remove cakes from pan.

FLUFFY VANILLA FROSTING

¾ cup butter
½ tsp. vanilla
dash salt
6 cups confectioners' sugar
1 egg white
2-3 Tbsp. milk
1-2 cups coconut for garnish

Cream butter, vanilla, salt and egg white. Add sugar and milk until frosting consistency. Assemble cake sprinkling coconut on top of frosting between layers and patting coconut on top and sides of cake when completely iced.

COCONUT CANDY
Ella Berger

1 8 oz. block cream cheese
1 stick margarine
8 oz. Angel Flake coconut
2¼-2½ lbs. confectioners' sugar
1 tsp. vanilla

Cream margarine and cream cheese. Add sugar, vanilla and coconut until stiff enough to work into small eggs. Let dry and roll in melted coating chocolate.

POTATO CANDY

1 baked potato
Confectioners' sugar
vanilla

Scoop the potato, while still warm into a mixing bowl. Mash the potato and add the sugar stirring and adding until the mixture can be kneaded with the hands. Knead well, keeping warm, add vanilla and form into small balls or shape like Easter eggs. They can be dipped in coating chocolate or sprinkled with cinnamon. For another variation roll out like pie dough, spread with peanut butter and roll up and slice. May be dipped in coconut.

"Baking the Bread"

In the era of the outdoor bake oven, baking was a major task. It was usually done on a Friday or Saturday so that the bread was fresh for use over the weekend. As many as 2 dozen loaves of bread and a dozen pies were baked each week.

To prepare the leaven or starter, the housewife took scrapings from the dough tray from the last baking, poured warm water over them, soaked, then melted lard and butter, warm milk, flour and the leaven were mixed in the dough trough. The dough was mixed and kneaded many times, flour added until it formed a smooth round ball. The dough trough was placed near an open fire in a fireplace to rise, and was kneaded some more and had some more raising. Portions were put into straw baskets or wooden bowls for final raising.

When the bake oven had the right temperature, the housewife shook the loaves out of the baskets on to a flat wooden pallet or peel with a long handle and deposited them on the hearth with a quick flip. When the loaves were baked she got each one back on the peel and brought them out to cool.

Many loaves had a diameter of 12 to 14 inches and were 3 or more inches high.

–Gladys Lutz

Summer

Fields turn from shimmering green to golden drifts as the first cutting of wheat is harvested. Hay is cut and baled and the sweet smell of freshly mown fields permeates the air. Country fairs host 4-H competitions and summer has taken hold in rural Pennsylvania.

Our vegetable gardens have matured to the point where tender skinned new potatoes may be side-harvested and we watch closely for the first signs of ripening tomatoes on the vine. The first sweet corn begs its way off the cob and into a savory pie shell with some onions and cream and a corn pie is born.

The wild treats are also at their peak in summer. Growing among the fencerows that bound the fields, wild black raspberries and wine berries ripen in abundance. While harvesting these treats may be a challenge due to their thorny nature, the scratches are worth it when we sit down to a slice of silky black raspberry custard pie. Jams and jellies are put up and all is well.

The Kutztown Folk Festival gets underway in early July. This fifty-plus year old tradition has worked its way into the blood of generations of local residents. Factories and businesses are closed and vacation time is planned around this nine-day event so those of us with roots in the traditions can present to our children and the many visitors, the customs, crafts and food of the Pennsylvania Dutch.

There is no excuse for leaving the festival hungry. Various local organizations open their stands for the event and create specialties like funnel cake, Dutch fried potatoes, sausage sandwiches, potato pancakes, apple dumplings, and roasted ox. The women of the local Granges stir up big pots of their best soups and at any given stand you may come across chicken corn noodle soup or one of a variety of renditions of potato chowders. There are also food halls run by local churches where visitors enjoy a full sit-down meal, served family style. The tables in these establishments groan with sweets and sours of all varieties, baskets of bread, and bowls of a variety of Pennsylvania Dutch specialties that may include chicken potpie, ham and green beans, pork and sauerkraut, fried sausages and scrapple. Be sure to save room for a slice or two of the many varieties of home baked pies that round out the meal.

Back at home, the fair weather Sundays of summer are often occasion for family gatherings or reunions. It's off to grandmothers house or a cool, wooded grove and everyone arrives with a special culinary contribution.

A FOURTH OF JULY PICNIC
Oven Fried Chicken

Fancy Iced Tea	Jane Dietrich's Potato Salad
Deviled Eggs	Baking Powder Biscuits
Dutch Cole Slaw	Folk Festival Vanilla Ice Cream
Bread and Butter Pickles	Sour Cherry Pie

GARY'S BREAD

A hearty, moist bread with an interesting flavor.

2 cups whole wheat flour
1/2 cup rye flour
5 1/2 cups white flour
3 oz. butter
1/2-1 tsp. salt
1/2 cup honey
1/2 cup unsulphered molasses
3 tsp. cocoa
1 packet yeast
2 3/4 cups milk
1/4 cup warm water to dissolve yeast

Heat milk to scalding. Add butter, salt, honey, cocoa and molasses. When milk is below 130 degrees add yeast that has been dissolved in water. In a large bowl, place whole wheat, rye and 3 1/2 cups white flour. Add milk mixture and mix thoroughly. Cover and let rise 1 1/2 to 2 hours or until dough doubles. Punch down and add 2 cups white flour, mix in thoroughly. No kneading is necessary. Dough should be stiff but pliable, add warm water if necessary. Place dough in two larger greased bread pans, let rise to about 1/2 to 3/4 inches above rim of pans. Bake for 30 minutes at 350 degrees or until bread "knocks done." After removing from oven, butter crust, let bread cool in pan for 45 minutes as it will unmold more easily.

OATMEAL BREAD

1 cup quick oatmeal
1/2 cup whole wheat flour
5 cups white flour
1/2 cup brown sugar
1 Tbsp. salt
2 Tbsp. margarine
2 cup boiling water
1 package dry yeast dissolved in 1/2 cup warm water

Combine in a large bowl the oatmeal, whole wheat flour, brown sugar and salt. Add margarine to 2 cups boiling water and stir into dry ingredients. When batter is lukewarm add dissolved yeast. Stir in 5 cups white flour and when stiff knead for 5-10 minutes. Place in a greased bowl and let rise in a warm place until doubled. Punch down and let rise again. Divide and shape into loaves and place in two greased 9x5x3 inch loaf pans. Bake at 350 degrees for 30-40 minutes. Cool on rack brushing with butter for soft crust.

POTATO BREAD

1 1/4 lb. russet potatoes
1/2 cup milk
2 tsp. yeast
1 tsp. sugar
4 cups flour
1 Tbsp. milk

Cook potatoes until tender. Drain potatoes saving 1/2 cup potato water. Add 1/4 cup cold milk to the potato water. Sprinkle yeast and sugar over the liquid and set aside in warm place for 15 minutes. Put potatoes in oven to dry for ten minutes. Peel potatoes and mash with masher, one potato at a time. Set aside to cool. Gradually beat yeast mix and potatoes together adding flour and salt 1/4 cup at a time. Knead in more flour if dough is sticky. Knead until smooth. Cover and let rise in a warm place until doubled. Sprinkle flour on risen dough and knead one minute adding more flour if necessary. Dough should be stiff. Butter 2 eight cup loaf pans. Cut dough in equal parts and shape into loaves in greased pans. Cover and let rise to top of pans. Bake at 350 degrees for 50 minutes. When cold, wrap in plastic bags and refrigerate.

CORN PIE

Summer

1 small onion, diced
3 cups corn
1 Tbsp. flour
1/2 pint heavy cream
3 Tbsp. butter
salt and pepper
two crust pie shell

Saute onion in butter, add corn and cook slightly. Sprinkle flour over corn and mix. Season with salt and pepper and add heavy cream. Pour into bottom crust. Add top crust, crimping sides. Slash top crust in several places to allow steam to escape. Bake at 400 degrees for 10 minutes and then lower temperature to 350 degrees for another 30 minutes or until crust is golden.

OYSTER CORN FRITTERS

2 cups fresh sweet corn cut from the cob
2 Tbsp. flour
2 eggs separated
½ tsp. salt
½ tsp. pepper

Lightly beat the egg yolks and combine in a large bowl with corn, flour, salt and pepper. In a separate bowl, beat the egg whites until just stiff. Fold the whites into the corn mixture and drop the batter by spoonfuls "the size of an oyster" onto a hot buttered frying pan or griddle. Use a spatula to flip the fritters once and brown the other side. Serve immediately.

This makes about 20 fritters for 4 to 6 servings as a side dish.

CORN FRITTERS

6 ears grated corn
3 eggs, beaten
2 Tbsp. flour
1 tsp. baking powder
pinch of salt

Mix all ingredients and fry in greased frying pan turning once until browned on both sides.

CUCUMBER SALAD

2 cucumbers, peeled and thinly sliced
1 small onion, thinly sliced
1 tsp. salt
1 Tbsp. cider vinegar
1 tsp. sugar
½ cup heavy cream
fresh ground pepper to taste

Toss the cucumbers and onions with the salt. Place in a colander and allow moisture to drain for 10 to 15 minutes. Put the cucumbers in a serving bowl and add the vinegar and sugar. Toss to coat. Pour the cream over the cucumbers and add the pepper to taste. Serve immediately or chill briefly before serving.

RED PEPPER AND CUCUMBER SALAD

2 large sweet red peppers, thinly sliced
2 cucumbers, thinly sliced
2 green onions, thinly sliced
2 Tbsp. olive oil
2 Tbsp. red wine vinegar
salt and pepper to taste
snipped chives to garnish

Combine peppers, cucumbers and onions. Whisk olive oil, vinegar, salt and pepper. Pour over vegetables and gently mix. Garnish with snipped chives.

GLORIA HAMM'S BLACK RASPBERRY JAM

Yields about 8 cups

2 quarts back raspberries, crushed to make 5 cups berries
6 1/2 cups sugar
1 package Sure Jell fruit pectin

Measure fruit into 6-8 quart pan. Place sugar in a separate bowl. Stir the fruit pectin into the fruit and bring mixture to a FULL ROLLING BOIL on high heat, stirring constantly. Stir in sugar quickly. Return to a full rolling boil and boil exactly one minute, stirring constantly. Remove from heat and skim off foam with a metal spoon.

Ladle into clean hot jars, filling to within 1/8 inch of top. Wipe jar rims and threads. Cover with flat lid that has been in pan of boiling water. Screw band on tightly. Invert jars five minutes, and then turn upright. Let stand at room temperature for 24 hours. Store in cool, dry, dark place up to a year. Refrigerate open jars up to three weeks.

STRAWBERRY JAM

Yields about 8 cups

2 quarts strawberries with stems removed; crush to make 5 cups berries
7 cups sugar

Proceed as for Black Raspberry Jam

Note: Bulk fruit pectin is much cheaper than packaged Sure Jell.

BEST TOMATO CATSUP

8 lbs. tomatoes
1 medium onion, chopped
1/4 tsp. cayenne
1/2 -1 cup sugar
1 cup white vinegar
1 1/2 tsp. whole cloves
1 1/2 inch stick cinnamon, broken
1 tsp. celery seed

Wash, peel, remove stem ends, core and quarter tomatoes. Let stand in colander to drain off excess liquid. In 8-10 quart kettle, mix tomatoes, onions and cayenne. Bring to boiling, cooking until tomatoes are soft, about 15 minutes. Stir occasionally. Put through a food mill or coarse sieve. Press to extract juice. Add sugar and return to kettle. Bring to boil and simmer briskly 1 1/2 -2 hours or until mixture is reduced by half.

Meanwhile, in a small saucepan, combine white vinegar, cloves, cinnamon and celery seed. Cover, bring to boiling, remove from heat and let stand. Strain vinegar mixture into tomato sauce. Discard spices. Simmer until desired consistency, about 30 minutes. Stir often to prevent sticking.

Pour hot catsup into hot jars leaving 1/2 inch of headspace. Cover with sterilized lids and process in a boiling water bath for 35 minutes. Makes 2 pints.

BREAD AND BUTTER PICKLES

1 gallon medium sized cucumbers
8 small white onions
1 green pepper
1 sweet red pepper
1/2 cup coarse salt
cracked ice
5 cups sugar
1 1/2 tsp. turmeric
1/2 tsp. ground cloves
2 Tbsp. mustard seed
2 tsp. celery seed
5 cups vinegar

Thinly slice cucumbers and onions. Cut peppers in narrow strips. Combine vegetables and salt and cover with cracked ice. Mix thoroughly and let stand for three hours. Drain.

Combine remaining ingredients; pour over cucumber mixture in an acid proof pot. Bring to boiling and seal in sterilized jars. Makes 8 pints.

SUMMER POTATO SALAD

2 1/2 lbs. small red skinned or "new" potatoes from your garden
1/4 cup olive oil
salt and pepper
2 Tbsp. whole grain mustard
2 ribs chopped celery
1 medium onion, chopped
1 sweet red, orange, or yellow bell pepper
1 red delicious apple, quartered, cored and diced
1/2 cup sour cream
1/2 cup mayonnaise
2 or 3 Tbsp. of assorted fresh herbs such as parsley, chives, tarragon or basil - chopped

Rinse the potatoes well to remove any garden dirt and place in a large pot of boiling salted water to cook. Leave the skins on the potatoes. Potatoes should be just soft but not overcooked. This will take about 20 minutes.

Meanwhile, chop the celery, onion, and pepper and set aside. Quarter, core, peel and dice the apple and place in a bowl of cold water with the juice of 1/2 lemon to prevent browning. Chop the fresh herbs and set aside.

When the potatoes are cooked, drain them in a colander and allow them to cool slightly. You may remove the skins if you like, or leave them intact for this salad. Cut the potatoes into bite size pieces and transfer to a large bowl. Dress with the olive oil, salt and pepper, and whole grain mustard and toss gently. Drain the diced apples thoroughly and add them to the salad with the rest of the chopped vegetables and the herbs. Combine the sour cream and mayonnaise, add to the salad and toss gently to coat. Taste and adjust seasonings as you wish. May be served warm or chilled for later use.

8 or more servings

DUTCH COLE SLAW

3 cups cabbage, finely shredded
1/2 cup carrot
1/4 cup green pepper, chopped
1/2 cup mayonnaise
1 Tbsps. sugar
1 Tbsps. cider vinegar
1/2 tsp. dry mustard
1/2 tsp. celery seed

Combine the cabbage, carrot, and pepper in a bowl and chill.

Combine the remaining ingredients to make the dressing. Pour the mixture over the cabbage and toss to combine. Chill well and serve.

6 to 8 servings

DEVILED EGGS

6 hard-boiled eggs
2 Tbsps. mayonnaise
1 1/2 tsps. whole grain mustard
1 green onion, very thinly sliced (slice a little of the green and keep separate from white)
a few leaves of fresh flat-leaf parsley, finely chopped, optional
freshly ground black pepper
salt to taste
paprika, optional

Carefully halve the eggs and scoop the yolks into a small bowl. Using a fork, mash the yolks well and add the mayonnaise and mustard and mix until a creamy consistency is reached. Stir in the chopped white part of sliced onion and most of the chopped parsley. Season to taste with salt and pepper. Spoon the filling back into the whites and garnish the eggs with the chopped green onion, parsley, and paprika if you are using it.

Generally, you need to get to the picnic early if you want to try a deviled egg. You may double, triple, or quadruple this recipe to help alleviate the disappointment of latecomers.

JANE DIETRICH'S POTATO SALAD

1 cup vegetable oil
1/2 cup cider vinegar
3 Tbsp. sugar
1 1/2 tsp. salt
1/2 tsp. paprika
1/2 tsp. dry mustard
1 crushed clove of garlic
6 medium potatoes
2 ribs thinly sliced celery
1 medium onion chopped
1 Tbsp. chopped parsley
3 hard boiled eggs - chopped
1/2 cup or more mayonnaise

Rinse the potatoes and place in a large pot of boiling salted water to cook. Leave the skins on the potatoes. Potatoes should be just soft but not overcooked. This will take about 20 minutes.

Meanwhile prepare a dressing for the salad by combining oil, vinegar, sugar, salt, paprika, mustard and garlic in a jar or other container with a tight fitting lid. Shake the ingredients and set aside.

When the potatoes are cooked, drain them in a colander and allow them to cool slightly. Pull off the skins when the potatoes are still warm but cool enough to handle. Cut the potatoes into bite size pieces and place in a large bowl. Gently toss the warm potatoes with 1/2 to 3/4 cups of the prepared dressing. Reserve the extra for another use (which is likely to be a second batch of this potato salad). Add the celery, onion, parsley, eggs and mayonnaise and toss gently with the potatoes. Add more mayonnaise if the salad seems too dry. This may be served immediately or prepared ahead and chilled in the refrigerator for later use. 8 or more servings

SCALLOPED TOMATOES

6 large tomatoes, peeled, seeded,
   cut into 1 1/3 inch pieces
1 small onion, finely chopped
1 tsp. salt
1/2 tsp. pepper
2 tsp. sugar
4 slices white bread, crusts removed,
   cut into 1/3 inch cubes
7 Tbsp. butter, melted

Toss the tomatoes, onion and seasonings together in a bowl. Scatter the bread crumbs on a baking pan, drizzle with 4 Tbsp. melted butter and toast in a 375 degree oven until golden brown, about 8-12 minutes. Add to the tomatoes, toss together and place in a buttered casserole. Drizzle with remaining butter. Cover tightly and bake for 35 minutes. Uncover and bake 10 minutes more.

Summer

FRIED TOMATOES WITH MILK GRAVY

¼ lb. sliced bacon
½ cup flour
¾ tsp. salt
⅛ tsp. pepper
5 large firm tomatoes
sugar

Fry bacon until crisp: remove from skillet and keep warm. Combine flour, salt and pepper in a pie plate. Cut tomatoes in ½ inch slices; dip both sides in flour. Fry in pan drippings until golden brown on both sides. Sprinkle a pinch of sugar on each slice. Serve with Milk Gravy.

MILK GRAVY

1½ Tbsp. flour
2½ Tbsp. bacon drippings
2 cups milk
salt and pepper

Brown flour in bacon drippings; gradually add milk. Season to taste with salt and pepper. Cook over low heat until thick, about eight minutes. Pour over tomatoes.

OVEN FRIED CHICKEN

3 eggs, beaten
5-6 cloves garlic, minced
2 Tbsp. chopped parsley
8 pieces of chicken
1 stick butter
2 cups bread crumbs

Combine egg, garlic and parsley in large bowl. Season with salt and pepper. Add chicken turning to coat. Cover and refrigerate three hours, turning occasionally.

Preheat oven to 350 degrees. Melt the butter in a 10x15 inch jelly roll pan. Drain the chicken and coat in the bread crumbs. Place chicken, skin side down in pan with the butter. Bake about 45 minutes until the chicken is golden brown, turning occasionally.

"Mixing the Shoo Fly Pies"

Shoo Fly pies are soundly Pennsylvania and there are different ways of making them. Not really pies, they were a poor man's cake, made in the earlier days with sorghum, later with molasses and brown sugar. There are two schools of thought about the proper way to bake them, some prefer their shoo fly pies gummy at the bottom and some do not.

Line 3 pie tins with rich pastry.

Crumbs:

The crumbs are made of flour, brown sugar and butter and lard.

Bottom:

The bottom is made of dark molasses (country kind or New Orleans molasses), hot water, and baking soda.

Dry Kind:

After lining the pie tin with pastry, take some of the crumbs and mix with the molasses mixture. Fill the pie tin with batter and scatter more crumbs over the top of the pie. Bake for half hour or a little longer.

Wet Bottom Kind:

After lining the pie tin with pastry, pour the molasses mixture evenly into the tin, then add the crumbs. Bake until firm.

–Gladys Lutz

MAE BITTNER'S SHOOFLY PIE

1 cup flour
3/4 cup brown sugar
1 Tbsp. Crisco
a pinch of salt

Mix dry ingredients with Crisco and reserve 1/2 cup for crumb topping.

1 cup molasses (King's syrup)
3/4 cup hot water
1 tsp. baking soda in a little water
1 egg, beaten

Mix liquids and add to unreserved crumbs to make a thin batter. Pour batter into 9 inch unbaked pie crust and put 1/2 cup crumbs on top. Bake at 400 degrees about 30-40 minutes. Test with toothpick.

SHOOFLY PIE

This technique for shoofly pie is for the classic wet-bottomed version.

1 1/4 cups flour
6 Tbsp. butter
1/4 cup granulated sugar
1/4 cup brown sugar
1/2 cup unsulphered molasses
1/2 cup golden table syrup (King's or Turkey)
1/4 tsp. cinnamon
1/4 tsp. nutmeg
1/2 tsp. vanilla
1/2 tsp. baking soda
1/2 cup hot water

Preheat the oven to 375 degrees.

Mix the crumbs by combining the flour and sugars and cut in the butter using a pastry blender or your fingers. Set aside.

Stir together the molasses, syrup, nutmeg and vanilla. Dissolve the baking soda in the hot water and stir into the molasses. Pour this mixture into a well-chilled piecrust and sprinkle all of the reserved crumbs evenly over the liquid.

Bake in the lower third of the oven for about 45 minutes until the crust and crumbs are nicely browned and the syrup has started to bubble through the topping a bit.

KRIS AMEY'S PEACH FRITTERS

2 eggs, separated
2/3 cup milk or liquid from fruit
1 Tbsp. melted butter or oil
1 cup flour
1/4 tsp. salt
1 Tbsp. sugar
4 ripe peaches, peeled and cut into small pieces

Beat egg yolks and add milk and melted butter. Add flour, salt and sugar.

If there is time, let batter rest in refrigerator two hours. Add two stiffly beaten egg whites and fruit. Fry in deep fat until golden brown. Yields 24 medium sized fritters.

FANCY ICED TEA

10 oranges
7 lemons
1 cup loose orange pekoe tea
3 cups sugar
1 bunch fresh mint

Bring five quarts of water to a boil in a large pot. Squeeze oranges and lemons into a large pitcher. Put orange and lemon rinds, mint and loose tea in boiling water. Stir in sugar. Remove from heat and let steep for one hour. Strain tea, squeezing rinds before discarding. Combine tea mixture and juice and chill over ice. Makes 5½ quarts.

EGG CUSTARD PIE

3/4 cup sugar
4 eggs
3 Tbsps. flour
a dash of nutmeg or cinnamon or grated lemon rind (optional)
3 cups hot milk

Preheat the oven to 350 degrees.

Mix the sugar, eggs, flour and nutmeg very well – 5 minutes or so. Add the hot milk and stir well into the eggs. Pour into pie shell and bake at 350 until set and nicely browned on top – about 45 minutes.

VARIATIONS

Sprinkle the unfilled pie shell with a little sugar, dot with butter and top with one cup of fresh berries before adding the custard. Some of the fruit will rise to the top – this is not a problem.

Stir one cup of coconut into the custard before filling the pie shell.

Sprinkle cinnamon sugar on the just set pie about half way through baking.

"Churning the Butter"

Until the middle of the 19th century and before the advent of the creamery, large amounts of butter were made in or near the springhouse.

After the cream was ripened, it was transferred to the churn. Sometimes carrot juice was added for additional color. The most common churns were the upright or dasher and the barrel churn. The churn was turned by hand. After churning about $1/2$ hour, the butter began to form. It was taken out of the churn into a tub and worked in cold water to remove the buttermilk. Then it was salted lightly, and reworked until all the buttermilk was removed.

If the butter was to be marketed, it was shaped into rolls or balls or molded and printed with butter molds, impressing designs on the butter. Sometimes, schmierkaess was made of the skimmed milk.

–Gladys Lutz

SOUR CHERRY PIE

½ cup sugar
½ cup brown sugar
2 Tbsp. flour
½ cup water or cherry juice
2 Tbsp. butter
3 cups pitted sour cherries

Preheat the oven to 350 degrees.

Mix the sugar, brown sugar, flour and water or cherry juice in a medium saucepan and cook over medium-low heat, stirring constantly, until the mixture thickens. Add the butter and cook a minute more. Stir in the cherries.

Dot a well-chilled piecrust with butter and sprinkle a little flour and sugar over it. Pour in the cherry filling, top with basic pie crumbs (page 22) and bake in the lower third of the oven for 35 to 45 minutes until the filling is bubbly and the crust and crumbs are nicely browned.

MRS. ELWOOD'S CAKE

This is an excellent cake to top with berries and whipped cream.

1½ cups flour
1 cup sugar
1 tsp. baking powder
pinch salt
2 eggs beaten in a one cup measure
milk, added to eggs to make 1 cup
½ cup melted butter
1 tsp. vanilla

Mix all ingredients and pour into a prepared loaf pan. Bake at 375 degrees for 45 minutes.

ANGEL FOOD CAKE

10-12 egg whites
1 1/4 tsp. cream of tartar
1/4 tsp. salt
1 tsp. vanilla extract
1/2 tsp. almond extract
1 1/4 cups sugar
1 cup flour

Preheat the oven to 350 degrees. Beat the egg whites, cream of tartar and salt in a large bowl until they form soft peaks. Add the vanilla and almond extracts. Then gradually add the sugar, beating until the whites are stiff, but not dry, and shiny. Sift the flour into the egg whites and fold into the mixture. Spoon into an ungreased 10 inch tube pan and bake until a toothpick inserted in the cake comes out clean, about 40 minutes. Invert the cake onto a cake rack and cool completely without removing the cake from the pan. When the cake is cool, run a knife around the edge and place on a serving platter.

KAREN'S CHOCOLATE CAKE

If you only use one chocolate cake recipe, this should be the one. It can be baked in two layers, a 9x13 cake pan, a tube pan or made into cup cakes. Baking times vary accordingly, but it is a very adaptable recipe.

2 eggs
2 cups sugar (for a variation you can use
    1 cup brown and 1 cup granulated)
1 cup sour milk
1 cup oil
2 1/2 cups flour
3/4 cup unsweetened cocoa
2 tsp. baking soda
1 cup hot coffee
1 tsp. vanilla

Beat eggs and add sugar. Slowly add oil. Stir baking soda into sour milk to dissolve and add flour and cocoa alternately with sour milk. Add hot coffee and vanilla. Batter will be thin. Pour into two greased and floured cake pans. Bake at 350 degrees for 30 minutes. 45 minutes for a 9x13 pan and 60 minutes for a tube pan. Cake is done when toothpick inserted comes out clean. Ice with your favorite frosting.

CHOCOLATE FUDGE FROSTING

This also makes a quick and easy hot fudge sauce for ice cream.

1 cup granulated sugar
3 Tbsp. cornstarch
1 pinch salt
1 cup water
2 squares unsweetened chocolate
1 tsp. vanilla

Mix sugar, cornstarch and salt in quart size microwave safe bowl. Add water and stir. Break up squares of chocolate and add to liquid mixture. Microwave on high five to seven minutes stirring often until chocolate melts and mixture thickens. When it is frosting consistency remove from microwave and add vanilla. Cool slightly and use on cakes or cupcakes. This can also be cooked on the top of a stove, but it takes forever.

PEANUT BUTTER FROSTING

2 cups confectioners' sugar
1 Tbsp. butter
1 cup peanut butter
milk to moisten

Beat butter, peanut butter and sugar. Add enough milk until soft enough for frosting consistency.

FOLK FESTIVAL VANILLA ICE CREAM

A big hit at the Kutztown Pennsylvania German Festival's summer kitchen, this ice cream can be used as a basis for many additions or flavors. Take advantage of the egg whites that are left over and try your hand at an angel food cake.

8 cups milk
8 cups heavy cream
2½ Tbsp. vanilla
2 cups sugar
16 egg yolks

Heat milk and cream. Beat eggs in mixer and add sugar. Add one cup of the heated milk mixture to the eggs to temper and add eggs to the rest of the heated milk and cream. Cook, stirring constantly until the mixture is thick enough to coat the back of a spoon. Strain and chill overnight. Churn and freeze according to your ice cream freezer directions. Makes 6 quarts. Can be divided for a 3 quart freezer.

PEACH ICE CREAM

2 lbs. ripe peaches
2 cups sugar
2 qts. heavy cream
pinch of salt
3 tsp. vanilla extract

Peel, slice and mash peaches. In a large bowl combine peaches and sugar and mash thoroughly. Add cream, salt and vanilla. Mix well. Freeze according to your ice cream freezer directions. Makes 2-3 quarts.

VERNETTE MEYER'S VANILLA ICE CREAM

6 eggs
3 1/3 cups sugar
6 cups heavy cream
7 1/2 cups milk
3/4 tsp. salt

Beat eggs and sugar until stiff. Add other ingredients and beat three minutes.
Freeze according to your ice cream freezer directions. Makes 6 quarts.

BLACK RASPBERRY SAUCE

You may substitute almost any fresh summer berry in this recipe but black raspberries are our favorite. This sauce is delicious on vanilla ice cream or added to the vanilla custard in your ice cream freezer and blended into the mix during the final minutes of churning.

3 cups fresh black raspberries
1/4 cup sugar (or more – to taste)
3 Tbsp. water
2 tsps. fresh lemon juice

Combine the berries, sugar and water in a medium saucepan and cook over medium low heat, stirring often, until the sugar dissolves, the berries break down, and the sauce begins to boil. Remove from the heat and stir in the lemon juice. Cool the sauce slightly and pour it through a fine mesh sieve into a bowl. Press on the berry solids to extract all the wonderful syrup.

Autumn

The cool nights of August are the first hints of the changing seasons in Albany Township. September brings a hint of color to the trees covering the ridges on the Blue Mountain. The last ears of sweet corn have been frozen. Frost determines the taste of that last tomato on the vine and fall crops like cauliflower, Brussels sprouts and turnips show up at the farmers' markets. The fall harvest has begun.

In the last part of the nineteenth century and well into the twentieth century, this area of Pennsylvania was noted for its potato farms. Everyone in the family was called upon to assist with the harvest. Before machinery and automatic harvesters this must have been grueling, back breaking work as the potatoes were manually picked up out of the overturned furrows and loaded into wagons for transport to potato cellars and rail heads for shipment to Philadelphia, New York and Pittsburgh markets. In those days just to mention "Lehigh Gravel Grown" potatoes was enough to insure a sale. The Schuylkill and Lehigh Branch of the Reading Railroad was reported to have handled more potatoes in a twelve mile stretch than any other railroad in the country.

While there are still potato farms in the area the major crops grown locally and harvested in the fall are soybeans and corn. There are also many orchards growing apples and pears. Cider is a very popular product of these orchards with purists still yearning for an unpasteurized drink made with a variety of apples.

The nip of cool fall air tends to shift life inside but there are still many wonderful opportunities to be outside for hayrides, bonfires and local Halloween parades. The food that accompanies these events represents a variety of choices from garden, field and orchard.

The Monday after Thanksgiving is the beginning of deer season in Pennsylvania. In many areas schools are closed and it is to some a greater holiday than the previous Thursday. Deer hunters are avid about their sport but also pay attention to the product of the harvest. When the deer are dressed and butchered the variety of meat products varies from summer sausage and scrapple to dried venison and the fresh cuts of meats that are frozen for later use. The most prized of these cuts, the tenderloin, can be made into a wonderful gourmet meal when marinated and grilled.

Thanksgiving is celebrated with a meal that is centered on a roast turkey, potato filling and pumpkin pie. Also popular in Pennsylvania Dutch country is dried corn, a vegetable that has been a part of the local cuisine since before our ancestors came to these shores.

THANKSGIVING DINNER

Roasted Squash Soup   Pan Browned Brussels Sprouts
Roast Turkey   Cranberry Orange Relish
Corn Bread Stuffing   Pumpkin Pie
Potato Filling   Hickory Nut Cake

"Drying the Sweet Corn"

The freshly pulled corn was husked and all the silk removed. It was steamed on the kitchen stove or the summerhouse stove until the "milk" was set. It was then cut off the cob, spread thinly on flat pans and at first was placed on a flat roof or on a bench to dry in the sun. The pan was usually covered with a thin loosely woven cloth to keep out the flies.

On those farms which had indoor or outdoor bake ovens, they were used to dry the corn, but with the introduction of the cook stoves and kitchen ranges, the corn was dried in the oven.

The dryhouse was used many a time to dry corn. This was a small building about 4 feet square and 6 feet high. Inside were trays which could be pulled out from the front. The bottom of the trays were constructed with thin wooden slats to hold the corn and allow the heat from the inside stove to pass up. Later, fine wire mesh was used. The corn was stirred occasionally and the trays were shifted. The trays were always in the upper part of the dryhouse, away from the stove. The stove was in the center of the building. Prior to the time, corn was placed on trays, a fire was started with fine wood. A steady temperature had to be maintained and not allowed to get too hot.

When dried, the corn was put into jars or bags for winter use. When it was to be used, it had to be soaked 1 to 3 hours or overnight and then stewed with milk, sugar, butter and salt or made into other dishes like dried corn pudding or dried corn and chestnuts.

–Gladys Lutz

CHICKEN CORN SOUP

1 chicken, 4 to 5 pounds, cut into 8 pieces
2½ to 3 quarts water, or as needed
1 large onion
8 to 10 black peppercorns
2 tsps. salt, or to taste
4 cups freshly cut or frozen corn kernels
3 celery stalks, diced with leaves
6 ounces wide egg noodles
freshly ground pepper
⅔ cup finely chopped fresh parsley
2 hard-cooked eggs, chopped

Place the chicken in soup pot with enough water to cover it. Bring to a boil and reduce the heat to a quick simmer. Skim any foam that may rise to the surface. Add the onion, peppercorns and salt.

Simmer gently but steadily, partly covered, for about 1½ hours or until the chicken is tender and falling from the bone.

Remove the chicken and trim and discard the bones, skin, and onion. Let the soup cool and skim most of the fat from the surface. Shred the meat and return it to the soup pot.

Puree half of the corn in a food processor and add it to the soup with the whole kernels, celery and noodles. Simmer gently until the corn and noodles are cooked. Season the soup with salt and pepper to taste. Stir in the parsley and serve, garnishing each portion with chopped egg.

8 to 10 servings

POTATO CORN CHOWDER

2 slices bacon
2 Tbsps. butter
½ cup chopped onion
½ cup chopped celery
2 medium potatoes, cubed
2 cups corn – fresh or frozen kernels
½ tsp. salt
¼ tsp. pepper
2 cups chicken broth
2 Tbsps. flour
2 cups milk

In a 3-quart saucepan fry the bacon until crisp. Remove the bacon and drain on a paper towel. Crumble the bacon and set aside.

Cook the onions, celery and potatoes in the bacon drippings until soft but not brown. Add the butter and melt. Sprinkle the flour over the vegetables in the pot and stir into the mixture to avoid lumps. Stir in the broth and milk and bring the chowder to a simmer. Add the corn. Season with salt and pepper to taste and simmer for 15 to 20 minutes until the potatoes are tender. Ladle into bowls and top with the crumbled bacon.

Makes 4 to 6 servings

ROASTED SQUASH SOUP

1 acorn squash – about 2 pounds
1 butternut squash – about 2 pounds
butter and brown sugar,
   salt and pepper for the squash
4 Tbsp. unsalted butter
1 large yellow onion - chopped
2 cloves garlic - finely chopped
4 cups chicken broth
1 cup heavy or light cream
¼ tsp. cinnamon
¼ tsp. ground ginger
¼ tsp. mace

Preheat oven to 400 degrees. Cut the squash in half and scoop out the membrane and seeds. Place skin side down on a baking sheet and place a dab of butter in the cavity of each piece. Sprinkle each half with a little brown sugar, salt, and pepper. Cover the pan with foil and roast for 45 minutes or more until the squash is tender. Remove from the oven and allow cooling so you can handle them.

While the squash is roasting, melt the butter in a soup pot and cook the onion and garlic over low heat until just softened- about 10 minutes. Add the chicken stock to onions and simmer for another 10 minutes. Scoop out flesh from the roasted squash and put in the soup pot. Discard the skins. Add salt and pepper to taste and continue simmering the soup for 20 minutes more.

Allow the soup to cool slightly and puree it, in batches, in a food processor or blender. Stir in the heavy cream and spices and serve hot with a dollop of sour cream and some fresh-snipped chives if available.

6 servings

HAM AND BEANS IN A CROCKPOT

2 lb. piece of ham, preferably with bone
2 lbs. fresh green or yellow beans
 or
2 bags frozen green or yellow beans
1 large onion

Place ham in crock pot, cover with beans and onion. Cook according to your crock pot's directions until beans are soft and ham comes off the bone and falls apart. Stir together before serving over mashed potatoes. If using fresh beans you may need to add some water to make a broth.

"Hunting Wild Turkeys"

Wild turkeys were once very plentiful all over temperate North America. If one was a skillful hunter years ago and knew how to slip up on them, he could find flocks of wild turkeys even near the Pa. Dutch farmsteads.

These birds were 3 feet tall and sometimes tipped the scale at 30 pounds. But they diminished rapidly as a result of intensive hunting.

In the fall the Dutch farmers would go out into their fields near the woodlands and shoot them not just for the sport of it, but to provide meat for the family.

Today, game commissions release and stock certain areas and hunting is allowed only at a certain time.

–*Gladys Lutz*

DOTTY BRETT'S CHICKEN POTPIE

3½ to 4 lbs. chicken
4 qts. Cold water
1 medium onion, diced
3 ribs celery
1 diced carrot
6 sprigs parsley
1 tsp. salt
½ tsp. black pepper
¼ tsp. poultry seasoning
2 cups flour
2 eggs
a pinch of salt
warm water
2 or 3 large potatoes – peeled
1 tsp. chopped parsley

Prepare chicken broth:

Place 3-4 lbs. of chicken - whole or parts - in 4 qts. of cold water. Bring slowly to a boil. Reduce heat and simmer for 30 minutes. Remove the scum.

Add 1 diced medium onion, 3 stalks celery, 1 diced carrot and 6 sprigs of parsley.

Continue to simmer. Add 1 tsp. salt and ½ tsp. black pepper, ¼ tsp. poultry seasoning. Taste and adjust seasoning.

Simmer for 2-3 hours. Remove chicken and cut it into small pieces. Keep warm.

Prepare Dough (while chicken is cooking):

Combine 2 Cups flour; 2 eggs; pinch of salt in bowl.

Mix with hands until crumbly. Add a few drops of warm water and form into a ball. Let it rest for 5 minutes, covered.

Knead ball until smooth.

Roll out on a lightly floured surface 1/16 th inch thick.

Cut into small, square pieces and let dry, 3-4 hours.

Finishing the potpie:

Bring the prepared chicken broth to a boil. Add potpie dough pieces slowly and return to a boil.

Add 2-3 potatoes, cut into slices, to the pot.

Continue to cook until potatoes and noodles are tender.

Add 1 tsp. chopped parsley.

Check seasoning and adjust.

Add reserved chicken pieces to the potpie and serve.

BREAKFAST CASSEROLE

1 lb. bulk sausage, sweet or hot
6 eggs
2 cups milk
1 tsp. salt
1 tsp. dry mustard
6 slices bread torn in small pieces
1½ cups shredded sharp cheddar cheese

Crumble and brown the sausage, drain and allow to cool. Butter a 9x13 inch glass baking dish and place sausage and bread on the bottom. Beat the eggs and milk together. Stir in the remaining ingredients and pour the mixture over the meat and bread. Cover tightly with foil or plastic wrap and refrigerate overnight. Bake uncovered at 350 degrees for 40-50 minutes.

Allow to rest a few minutes before cutting. Serves 6-8

CORN BREAD AND BACON STUFFING

2 8.5 oz. packages of Jiffy corn muffin mix
6 or 8 pieces of stale white bread - cubed
1/2 pound bacon cut into small pieces
1/4 cup butter
2 medium onions, chopped
3 ribs celery, diced
1 cup shredded Monterey Jack cheese
1 bunch green onions, finely sliced
1/4 cup chopped parsley
1 or more cups chicken broth or cream
  or a combination
salt and pepper to taste

Prepare the cornbread according to the package directions. When it is cool, break it up into a large bowl with the cubed white bread and set aside.

Fry the bacon in a large skillet until it is crisp and remove it from the pan to paper towels to drain. Add the butter, onions and celery to the pan and cook over medium heat until just softened. Add this to the cornbread in the bowl along with the cheese, the green onion, the bacon pieces, and the parsley. Toss to combine.

Moisten the mixture with the stock or cream and mix until combined. If necessary, add more liquid until the stuffing is nicely moistened.

A very versatile stuffing, this may fill your thanksgiving bird, or you may prefer to bake it separately at 350 degrees in a buttered casserole, or use it to stuff pork chops.

VENISON TENDERLOIN WITH APPLE BUTTER MARINADE

1-2 lb. venison tenderloin
1/2 cup apple butter
2 Tbsp. cider vinegar
1/4 cup oil
2 tsp. grated horseradish
1 tsp. chopped fresh rosemary
2 cloves minced garlic
salt and pepper

Whisk the marinade ingredients together. Place the tenderloin in a glass pan and pour the marinade over the meat. Marinate two to four hours in the refrigerator turning several times. Grill over hot coals or gas grill about twenty minutes turning once. Let rest ten minutes under tented foil, slice and serve. Marinade may be heated and served with the meat.

"Stomping the Sauerkraut"

The chief fermented Pa. German Dutch food was fermented shredded cabbage known as sauerkraut. Cabbages were easily grown and as soon as the heads matured they were taken on the porch, cellar, or other convenient place to be made into sauerkraut.

First, the cabbage heads were quartered then grated on the "hovel" and shredded. It was put into a large crock about 3 inches deep, and salted lightly. Next the kraut was pounded with a stomping tool until all juices were squeezed out. Layer upon layer of kraut was added, salted, then stomped until the salty juices rose. When the crock was full it was covered with a cloth, covered again with a round board or slate stone and left in the cellar to ferment a few weeks.

When ready to eat, it was soaked in fresh water to remove some of the salt. The kraut was cooked with pork and eaten with mashed potatoes, dumplings with sauerkraut, sauerkraut wit brisket of beef, or pig's knuckles.

–Gladys Lutz

PEPPER CABBAGE

1 large head of cabbage
1 medium bell pepper – any color
1 medium onion
1 cup sugar
1 tsp. salt
1 tsp. dry mustard
1 tsp. celery seed
1 cup vinegar
2/3 cup vegetable oil

Trim, core and quarter the cabbage. Chop fine, without pureeing by pulsing the cabbage in the bowl of a food processor. Do the same with the bell pepper and the onion and transfer to a large bowl. Do not over-process! You do not want a watery mess.

Mix the rest of the ingredients in a saucepan and bring to a boil, stirring, to dissolve the sugar. Cool to room temperature and pour over the cabbage. Cover and refrigerate. Serve chilled.

CRANBERRY ORANGE RELISH

Makes 4 cups
4 cups fresh cranberries
2 oranges, quartered with seeds removed, do not peel
2 cups sugar

Process fruits in food processor. Stir in sugar and chill. For a variation add 2 Tbsp. finely minced crystallized candied ginger.

BEET RELISH

2 cups chopped cooked beets
1 cup chopped red bell pepper
2 cups chopped cabbage
2 tsp. horseradish
1 1/2 cups cider vinegar
1/2 cup chopped onion
1 cup sugar
2 tsp. salt

Combine all of the ingredients in a large saucepan and bring to a boil for 5 to 10 minutes. Chill and serve cold. This relish may be made in larger quantities and sealed in canning jars if you are so inclined.

PAN-BROWNED BRUSSEL SPROUTS

1 1/2 Tbsp. unsalted butter
1 Tbsp. olive oil
2 large cloves garlic, thinly sliced
1/2 lb. brussel sprouts,
   trimmed and halved lengthwise
2 Tbsps. Pine nuts or pecans
salt and freshly ground pepper

Melt 1 Tbsp. butter with oil in a cast iron skillet over moderate heat. Add the garlic and cook, stirring, until pale golden, about three minutes. Remove from pan and reserve.

Reduce the heat to low and add the brussel sprouts, cut sides down, in one layer. Sprinkle with the nuts and salt to taste. Cook, uncovered, without turning, until sprouts are crisp-tender and undersides are golden, 10-15 minutes. Transfer the sprouts to a serving plate leaving nuts in the pan. Add remaining 1/2 Tbsp. of butter and cook nuts over moderate heat, stirring about one minute until evenly browned. Stir in garlic and spoon over brussel sprouts and season with pepper.

GREEN BEAN SALAD

6 slices bacon, fried and crumbled
1 pound fresh green beans or
   1 pint cooked green beans
1/4 tsp. salt
1/2 cup celery, chopped fine
2 to 3 hard-cooked eggs, chopped
1 small onion, chopped fine

Fry the bacon until crisp, drain on paper towel and crumble. Set aside. Add the green beans, a small amount of water, and salt to bacon drippings. Cook the beans until just tender.

Transfer the beans to a bowl and toss in the celery, eggs, and onion. Stir in the dressing and serve warm, or chill the salad for later use.

DRESSING

1 Tbsp. onion, grated
1/3 cup vinegar
2 Tbsp. sugar
1/2 tsp. salt
a dash each of pepper, paprika, and garlic powder

Heat the ingredients in a saucepan, stirring occasionally, just until boiling. Pour over the green beans while hot or chill and serve over the cold bean salad.

GREEN BEANS WITH TOMATOES

1 quart cooked green beans
4 Tbsps. butter
1/4 cup onion, chopped
1/4 green pepper, diced
1 cup peeled, chopped, fresh tomatoes
1 tsp. flour
1 tsp. salt
1/8 tsp. pepper

Melt the butter and sauté the green beans, onion, and green pepper until lightly browned.

Mix the flour, salt, and pepper with tomatoes and add to the green bean mixture and cook slowly for 6 to 8 minutes. Serve warm.

6 to 8 servings

BRAISED RED CABBAGE

Excellent as a side dish with roast pork or pork chops filled with cornbread bacon stuffing.

1 lb. bacon cut into 1 inch piece
2 cups chopped onions
1 3 lb. head of red cabbage, cored and finely chopped
2 tart apples, cored and cut into cubes
3/4 cup dry red wine or apple cider
3/4 cup red wine vinegar or cider vinegar
3 Tbsp. dark brown sugar, packed
2 tsp. caraway seeds
1 tsp. dried thyme leaves
1/2 tsp. each salt and fresh ground pepper

Cook the bacon in a large deep skillet or Dutch oven over low heat for 15 minutes. Add the onions and cook 10 minutes more until they have wilted. Add the remaining ingredients and combine well.

Cover the skillet and cook over medium heat for 1 1/4 hours, stirring occasionally. If necessary, add more liquid to prevent scorching. Serve hot.

8 servings

BARLEY CASSEROLE

1 16 oz. can stewed tomatoes
³/₄ cup quick barley
1 cup boiling water
4 Tbsp. butter
²/₃ cup sharp cheese, grated
1 large onion, chopped
¹/₈ tsp. curry powder
¹/₂ tsp. celery salt
1 tsp. salt
fresh ground pepper

Mix all ingredients in a buttered casserole. Bake one hour at 325 degrees or until barley is soft and mixture thickens. It can be held in turned off oven until ready to eat.

POTATO ONION PIE

2 lbs. potatoes
3 medium onions
1 cup milk
¹/₂ cup shredded cheese
salt and pepper to taste

Peel potatoes and onions and slice thinly. Butter a 9 inch pie pan and layer potatoes, onions, salt and pepper. Pour milk over top and let it seep in. Cover with cheese and bake 45 minutes until brown and bubbly.

APPLE PIE

1 prepared pie crust - chilled
6 to 8 apples (mixing varieties works best)
2 Tbsp. flour
¹/₄ cup brown sugar
¹/₄ cup granulated sugar
¹/₂ tsp. cinnamon
¹/₄ tsp. grated nutmeg
2 Tbsp. melted butter
extra butter, cinnamon, and sugar for the pie crust

Sprinkle the pie shell with the cinnamon and sugar, and dot with the butter.

Peel, core, and quarter the apples and place them in a mixing bowl that is large enough to hold them comfortably. Sprinkle the apples with the flour, both sugars, cinnamon, nutmeg and butter and toss to combine the ingredients. Transfer the apples to the chilled crust and bake in the lower third of a 375 degree oven for about 45 minutes or until the filling is bubbly and the apples are tender when pierced with a fork. If you prefer a crumb pie, prepare the recipe for basic pie crumbs and sprinkle the crumbs over the pie before baking.

APPLE BUTTER CAKE

¾ cup butter
1¼ cups sugar
3 eggs
1½ cup apple butter
½ cup buttermilk
3 cups flour
1½ tsp. baking soda
¾ tsp. each salt, cinnamon,
  ground cloves and nutmeg

Cream butter and sugar. Beat in eggs one at a time. Combine dry ingredients. Combine apple butter and buttermilk. Mix dry ingredients and liquids into butter mixture alternately. Pour into 2 nine inch cake pans and bake at 350 degrees for 35 to 40 minutes.

APPLE CRISP

4 cups tart apples
2 Tbsp. lemon juice
½ cup flour
½ cup brown sugar
¼ cup butter
1 cup rolled oats
1 tsp. cinnamon
¼ tsp. nutmeg

Peel and slice apples into a nine inch square pan. Drizzle with lemon juice and stir. Mix remaining ingredients into crumb mixture and spread over the apples. Bake at 375 degrees about 30 minutes or until apples are soft and crumbs are brown. Serve hot or cold with ice cream.

PUMPKIN PIE

Frances Wright Trexler

3 cups thick stewed pumpkin
2 cups milk
1 cup sugar
1 tsp. salt
4 eggs, beaten
1 Tbsp. ground ginger
2 Tbsp. butter
cinnamon

Add all ingredients, except cinnamon, to beaten eggs. Pour into two large unbaked pie shells and sprinkle with cinnamon. Bake at 400 degrees for 10 minutes and lower oven to 350 degrees. Bake about 30 minutes more or until inserted knife comes out clean.

Very good served with cranberry sauce.

ELSIE SNYDER'S LEMON STRIP PIE

SWEET DOUGH

1 cup flour
1/4 cup softened butter
1/3 cup brown sugar
1/2 tsp. baking soda
1/2 tsp. baking powder
pinch of salt
1 egg
milk to moisten

FILLING

1 lemon, grated rind and juice
2 eggs
1/2 cup brown sugar
1/2 cup white sugar
1 tsp. butter
1 cup water

For the sweet dough: Cream the butter and sugar. Add the egg, baking soda, baking powder and salt. Gradually add the flour. Add enough milk to bind the dough. It should be stiff for rolling. Form into a ball and press down into a thick circle. Chill in the refrigerator for better rolling.

For the filling: beat the eggs and the sugars for three minutes; add butter, grated lemon, lemon juice and the water. Pour into an unbaked nine inch pie crust. Leave extra dough around the edge of the pie crust. Criss-cross strips of the sweet dough over the top of the filling. Fold the pie crust rim over the sweet dough and crimp. Filling will be thin, so strips may sink, but they will rise up as they are baking. Bake at 375 degrees for ten minutes. Lower temperature to 350 degrees and bake 35-40 minutes more until golden brown.

LEMON SPONGE PIE

1 cup granulated sugar
2 Tbsp. melted butter
3 egg yolks
2 Tbsp. flour (rounded)
1/2 tsp. salt
1 1/2 cups milk
1 lemon, juice and grated rind
3 egg whites, beaten

Cream the sugar, butter, egg yolks, flour and salt. Add the lemon juice, grated rind, and milk. Beat the egg whites until fluffy but not dry and fold them into the lemon filling. Pour the filling into a well-chilled unbaked piecrust and bake at 350 degrees for about 45 minutes. The top should be golden brown.

"Schnitzing and Cooking Apple Butter"

Apples were used in two ways to make apple butter. They were schnitzed and some were made into cider. The apples were crushed in a press and then the juice was put into kegs to ferment. When fermented, the cider was put into a large copper kettle over a fire, was boiled down to ½ of its quantity, water was added and boiled again. Sliced schnitz were added with sassafras. Then it was stirred and stirred so that it would not stick to the bottom and when cooked about 6 hours, sugar, cloves, and cinnamon were added. When the apple butter formed a simple heap in a dish, it was dipped into earthen crocks and when cold, taken up to the attic and stored for winter use.

Apple butter was eaten spread on bread with butter, but more often smearkaess and apple butter were spread on the bread.

Apples were pared, cored, and quartered or cut into eighths. They were dried, put into paper bags, large glass jars or other containers for winter use. They were most frequently used to make schnitz und knepp or schnitz pie. In both cases the schnitz had to be soaked overnight and then boiled.

–Gladys Lutz

GINGERBREAD

2 eggs
3/4 cup brown sugar
3/4 cup molasses
3/4 cup melted butter
2 1/2 cups flour
2 tsp. baking soda
1 1/2 tsp. cinnamon
2 tsp. ginger
1/2 tsp. nutmeg
1/2 tsp. baking powder
1 cup boiling water

Beat eggs and add sugar, molasses and melted butter. Mix well. Add sifted dry ingredients until well blended. Add boiling water and stir until evenly mixed. Pour into greased 9x13 inch pan. Bake at 350 degrees for 30-40 minutes. Serve warm with whipped cream.

Variation: Bake this over a campfire using a cast iron dutch oven. Pour one quart of applesauce in the bottom of the oven and add the gingerbread batter. Bake until done. Time may vary depending on temperature of the coals.

HICKORY NUT CAKE

1 1/2 cups white sugar
1/2 cup shortening
2 cups sifted all-purpose flour
2 Tbsps. baking powder
1/2 tsp. ground nutmeg
1/4 tsp. salt
1 cup finely chopped hickory nuts
1 cup milk
3 egg whites

Preheat the oven to 350 degrees. Grease and flour 2 - 9 inch round cake pans. Sift the flour, baking powder, nutmeg and salt together and set aside.

In a large bowl, cream sugar and shortening until light and fluffy. Add the flour mixture alternately with the milk. Stir in the nuts.

In a separate clean bowl, whip the egg whites until stiff peaks form. Quickly but gently fold the whites into the batter.

Divide the batter evenly between the 2 pans. Bake at 350 degrees for 25 to 30 minutes, or until a toothpick inserted into the cake comes out clean.

COOKED ICING
"Cookie Lightcap"

Like so many recipes that have been passed down through the generations, there are many variations on this recipe. "Cookie" relates that her mother, Ethel George, called it "fried icing" because she made it in a cast iron pan on the cookstove. The recipe may be made in a saucepan on the top of the stove, but you must stir it continually as it cooks as it burns easily. It is presented here as a microwave version for the "modern" cook.

- 1 cup whole milk
- 2 Tbsp. cornstarch
- 1 cup light brown sugar
- 1/4 cup cold butter
- 1 cup finely chopped hickory nut pieces
- 1/2 tsp. salt
- 1/2 tsp. vanilla

In a microwave safe container, (glass preferably) combine the milk and cornstarch and stir to dissolve. Stir in the brown sugar and add the cold butter cut into pieces. Microwave on medium heat setting until the icing begins to boil, stirring every couple of minutes. Set microwave to low and continue cooking for 5 to 8 minutes until the frosting thickens to the point where it coats a spoon. Remove from the microwave and stir in 1/2 tsp. salt, 1/2 tsp. vanilla, and chopped nutmeats. Cool to room temperature and pour over cake layers like a glaze, or cool completely, refrigerate, then bring back to room temperature and spread it on the layers as an icing.

SPICE CAKE

- 1 cup butter
- 2 cups sugar
- 4 eggs
- 1 cup sour milk or 1 1/2 cups apple sauce
- 3 cups flour
- 1 tsp. baking soda
- 1 tsp. cream of tartar
- 2 tsp. cocoa
- 1 tsp. each of cloves, nutmeg and cinnamon

Cream butter and sugar. Add eggs one at a time. Mix in milk or applesauce and beat until smooth. Add dry ingredients. Pour into three cake pans and bake at 350 degrees for 30-35 minutes. Ice with your favorite frosting.

"Smoking the Meats"

Because of the lack of refrigeration during earlier days, much of the meat such as hams, shoulders, bacon, sausage, baloney, dried beef and tongue were placed in the smokehouse to be smoked over a smoldering fire. Some farmers brine-cured their meat before smoking, others dry-cured the meat.

A slow wood fire was started in the fireplace in the smokehouse and was smothered with wood chips or sawdust to make it smoke. The fire had to be kept at an even temperature. The wood was hickory or apple.

The meats were hung with iron hooks over poles or tree arms about 6 to 8 feet above the fire and was sometimes shielded by a sheet of metal.

The length of time the meat was allowed to remain in the smokehouse was largely up to the individual. Some liked the meats smoked hard, others not. The small pieces were usually smoked 24 to 36 hours when the fire was kept burning steadily. The larger pieces were smoked longer but usually not longer than a week.

Hams and shoulders had to be seasoned after curing and smoking from 30 to 60 days before used, bacon was seasoned 10 to 15 days before used.

–Gladys Lutz

Winter

As the days grow shorter and Christmas approaches everyone seems to enjoy the warmth of the kitchen and preparations for the holidays. Life slows down. There are no gardens to tend and the outside field work has ended for the farmers.

Many of the traditional Christmas customs celebrated by Americans today came from Germany. Foremost among them is the Christmas tree. Christmas trees have been a cash crop in the northern Berks, Schuylkill County region for at least the last fifty years.

And they are still decorated locally with cookies, candy canes, popcorn strands and cranberries.

Christmas gives those of us who like to cook and bake the excuse to try new things and serve them to our guests. Winter, in general, seems to be the season when folks tend to spend time indoors and use food as a link to their pasts. It is also an excellent opportunity to try new recipes and entertain friends on those cold, snowy nights.

A snow day home from school always affords a chance, when time is available, to bake bread or make a batch of doughnuts. The true "winter pastry" is the fastnacht (fast night), a potato based yeast doughnut fried in lard on Shrove Tuesday to celebrate the beginning of Lent and the end of eating leavened breads for forty days until Easter. Those of us born and raised in Albany Township and surrounding areas are particular about our fastnachts. Some eat them with sweet molasses while others glaze them or use powdered sugar. Whatever the tradition you can tell a true Berks Countian by their affinity for these solid fried pieces of dough. It seems to be a food you need to be "born into" to truly appreciate.

In winter caution is thrown to the wind and comfort foods laden with all the things we shouldn't eat are consumed. Just like the groundhog, the mascot of the "Grundsow Lodges," we will emerge in spring to check things out and decide if we want to hibernate for six more weeks or crawl right out and embrace the coming of the eternal spring season.

CHRISTMAS MORNING BREAKFAST
Mary Wright's One-Rise Cinnamon Rolls
Creamed Dried Beef
Baking Powder Biscuits
Home Fried Potatoes
Fresh Fruit

DINNER BY THE FIRE
Oyster Stew
Venison Tenderloin with Apple Butter Marinade
Creamy Scalloped Potatoes
Braised Red Cabbage
Evelyn Dunkelberger's Molasses Coconut Pie

CREAMED DRIED BEEF

A country staple, this dish is served as breakfast, lunch, or dinner.

4 Tbsps. butter
1/4 pound dried beef, thinly sliced
1/2 cup water
4 Tbsps. flour
2 1/2 cups milk

Brown the butter in a heavy skillet. Add the shredded pieces of dried beef and brown lightly. Add the water and boil until it is evaporated. This step tenderizes the beef.

Sprinkle the flour over the beef and cook for a minute or two. Slowly stir in the milk and cook over low heat, stirring constantly. Continue cooking until smooth and thickened.

You may serve this over baked potatoes, biscuits, or toast. Makes 4 servings

HAM AND STRING BEANS

3 to 4 lb. ham or ham hocks
1 onion, peeled and quartered
3 or more cups water
2 Tbsp. melted butter
1 Tbsp. flour
2 quarts fresh green beans, washed and trimmed
4 medium size potatoes, peeled and quartered

Place the ham and onion in a large saucepan or soup pot and cover with the water. Cover the pot and cook over medium heat for an hour or more until the ham is tender and the delicious broth that this dish is noted for has developed. At this point, you should be able to easily shred the ham in the pan. After doing this, whisk the flour into the melted butter in a small bowl. Retrieve some of the broth from the pot and whisk this into the flour mixture. Stir the mixture back into the broth in the pot and add the green beans and potatoes. Cook for another half hour or until the beans and potatoes are tender. Add more water as necessary.

MARINATED ROAST VENISON TENDERLOIN

1/2 to 1 cup apple cider vinegar
1 tsp. peppercorns
1 onion, thinly sliced
1 2-3 lb. venison tenderloin
2 Tbsp. butter

Combine vinegar, peppercorns and onions. Marinate tenderloin for 24 hours, turning 4 times. Preheat oven to 550 degrees. Dry tenderloin with a paper towel, rub with butter and place on roasting pan. Reduce heat to 350 degrees and roast for 20 minute per lb. or until meat thermometer registers 140 degrees. Let venison rest for 10 minutes before carving. Serves 6-8

PORK AND SAUERKRAUT

Chickens scratch backwards but hogs root forward. It only stands to reason that to insure a successful new year, this is the dish to serve on New Year's Day. Accompany with plenty of mashed potatoes or potato filling.

1 pork roast, about 4 to 5 lb.
salt and pepper
1 Tbsp. oil
2 large bags or cans of sauerkraut (bagged sauerkraut is generally less salty than canned)
1/2 cup applesauce
1/4 cup brown sugar

Heat the oil in a large Dutch oven or a large, deep, heavy skillet. Season the pork roast with salt and pepper and brown the meat briefly on all sides. Add a cup or more of water to the pork in the pan, cover, and cook over low heat for 1 1/2 hours. Add the sauerkraut, applesauce and brown sugar. Cover and simmer for another hour or more until the roast is tender and falling apart. During this final cooking, check occasionally to see that there is still liquid remaining and add water as necessary.

Cooking variations:

Roast the pork in the oven at 350º for about an hour and a half. Reduce the oven temperature to 300 and add the sauerkraut, applesauce and sugar. Roast for an hour more, checking occasionally to make sure the pan has not dried out.

This is also a good crock-pot meal. Just add everything at once and cook for about 6 or 7 hours on low.

8 servings

STUFFED PIG'S STOMACH

While not for everyone, this is truly a classic. It is definitely delicious and worth the effort. Pig stomachs are available cleaned and ready to use at local butcher shops in Pennsylvania Dutch country.

1 large pig's stomach, well cleaned of all fat
1 pound fresh sausage, cut into 1/2-inch slices
1 pound smoked sausage, cut into 1/2-inch slices
6-8 medium potatoes,
**   peeled and cut into 1/2-inch cubes**
2 medium onions, coarsely chopped
2 Tbsps. fresh parsley, chopped
Salt and pepper to taste
3 Tbsps. flour
2 cups of chicken stock or water

Mix together sausages, potatoes and onions. Add parsley, salt and pepper. Sew the small opened end of the stomach with cooking string to close. Stuff the sausage mixture into the stomach, pressing well with each addition. When all of the stuffing has been placed inside, sew the opening closed.

Place the stuffed stomach in a shallow roasting pan. Roast in a preheated 350° oven until the potatoes are tender – about 2 hours - check potatoes by inserting a thin sharp knife into the middle of the stuffed stomach. Baste about every 20 minutes with water or pan juices.

Transfer the stomach from the roasting pan to a serving platter. Drain off most of the fat from the pan and place the pan on a burner on the stovetop. Make gravy by whisking the flour into the remaining fat and brown bits in the pan. Add the stock and continue whisking until the gravy begins to boil and thicken. Taste the gravy and adjust seasonings. To serve, slice the stomach into 1 inch thick slices and pass the gravy separately. Serves 6 to 8

OYSTER STEW

1 quart of milk
1 pint stewing oysters
2 Tbsp. butter
1 tsp. pepper

In a 2-quart saucepan heat the milk just to the boiling point.

In a frying pan melt the butter and brown it. Drain the oysters; then add them one at a time to the browned butter. Cook the oysters in the butter for just 2 or 3 minutes – do not overcook! Add the pepper.

Add the oysters and butter to the hot milk and serve at once. 4 servings

BAKED SAUERKRAUT & CHOPS

1 large can of sauerkraut
2 apples, peeled, sliced
½ cup brown sugar
4 to 6 pork chops
salt and pepper

Mix the sauerkraut, apples, and brown sugar. Place the mixture in a 13x9 inch glass baking dish or a large casserole. Sprinkle about ¼ cup of water over the sauerkraut.

Season the pork chops with salt and pepper and brown lightly in a frying pan with a ½ tablespoon of oil. Arrange the pork chops on top of the sauerkraut mixture and cover the baking dish with foil. Bake for 1 hour at 350°. Remove the cover for the last 10 minutes of baking. Serve the dish with mashed potatoes and applesauce. Serves 4 to 6

CREAMY SCALLOPED POTATOES

1 Tbsp. unsalted butter
3 cups half-and-half
4 cloves garlic, smashed
3 pounds Russet potatoes,
    peeled and sliced ⅛ inch thick
Salt and freshly ground white pepper

Preheat the oven to 350°F. Butter a 6-cup gratin dish or baking dish 1½ to 2 inches deep.

Place the half-and-half in a 3-quart saucepan. Add the garlic and potatoes and bring to a simmer. Season with salt and pepper. Simmer for 5 minutes, and then transfer to the prepared gratin dish.

Bake for about 40 minutes, until the top is browned nicely and the potatoes are tender.

Note: You may substitute beef or chicken stock for all or part of the cream for a lighter dish.

Yield: 6 Servings

BASIC MASHED POTATOES

2 pounds potatoes
1 cup milk
6 Tbsp. butter
Salt and pepper to taste

Start a large pot of boiling salted water. Peel and quarter the potatoes and add to the pot. Make sure all of the potatoes are covered with water. Cook for 15 to 20 minutes until the potatoes are fork tender. Drain the liquid, add the milk, butter, salt and pepper and mash until light and fluffy adding more milk if the potatoes seem too dry.

"Serving the Pig Stomach"

Several butcherings took place on a Pennsylvania German farm during the fall and winter. It was considered a sin to waste anything – so practically everything of the pig was made to use except the squeal. As a result, even the pig's stomach was eaten.

After the stomach was thoroughly cleaned, it was soaked in cold salt water overnight. Then diced potatoes, onions, pork ribs, parsley, coriander, salt and pepper were mixed. This mixture was spooned into the pig's stomach, not too full for fear of splitting. It was sewn up with a strong string. The stomach was pricked with a carving knife here and there to allow the steam to escape. Sometimes, fresh or smoked sausage, hamburger or pork chops were used instead of the ribs.

Usually it was cooked in a suitable utensil about 2 to $2^1/_2$ hours, then fried in a buttered pan until golden brown. Or, it was put in the oven and baked until brown.

To serve, the stomach was placed on a large platter, surrounded with sprigs of parsley and other meat fried separately. It was sliced through into portions and served. Many a time it was served on New Year's Day.

–Gladys Lutz

POTATO FILLING

6 potatoes, peeled and cut
2 ribs celery, finely chopped
1 onion, finely chopped
1 cup bread cubes
1 stick butter
2 Tbsp. fresh parsley
1 egg
½ - 1 cup milk
salt and pepper to taste

Boil potatoes in salted water. While potatoes are boiling, sauté the onions and celery with the butter until soft and browned. Add the bread cubes, parsley, salt and pepper and more butter, if necessary. Drain and mash the potatoes using the milk and the egg. Add the sauté and mix well. Place in a buttered casserole and bake at 350 degrees until browned and heated through.

RAW POTATO PANCAKES

3 medium sized raw potatoes,
    peeled and coarsely grated
2 eggs, separated
1 ½ Tbsp. flour
½ tsp. baking powder
1 tsp. salt
butter for frying

Beat the egg yolks and stir in the grated potatoes. Combine the flour, baking powder and salt and mix into the potatoes. Beat the egg whites until soft peaks form and fold them into the potato mixture. Melt the butter in a skillet and spoon about 2 tablespoons of the potato mixture for each pancake into the hot butter. Brown on both sides. Serve at once with applesauce and sausage with gravy.

Makes about 12 pancakes.

SIMPLE POT ROAST

1 3-4 lb. chuck roast
2 onions, chopped in large pieces
3-4 potatoes, quartered
4-5 carrots, cut in two inch pieces
flour
salt and pepper to taste
cooking oil
1 can tomatoes, optional

Dredge roast in flour and salt and pepper. Heat cooking oil in a heavy skillet or Dutch oven and brown the meat on all sides. Add the onions and cover the meat about ¾'s of the way with water and add the canned tomatoes if you wish. Cook, covered over medium low heat for 2-3 hours until tender. Add potatoes and carrots, raising heat slightly and cook until the vegetables are tender. Remove meat and vegetables and add

3 Tbsp. of flour that has been shaken in a jar with about ½ cup of water. Add to pan juices and whisk and cook until gravy thickens. Season with salt and pepper. Slice meat and serve with the vegetables and gravy. Don't forget the bread for gravy bread!

SAUSAGE WITH GRAVY

1 lb. bulk pork sausage
1 small onion, finely chopped
1 Tbsp. flour
1 cup beef or chicken broth

Shape the sausage into 6 or 8 flat cakes. Place the cakes in a skillet over medium low heat and cook slowly - turning once - to brown sausages on both sides. Remove the cakes to a hot platter and keep warm. Drain off all but about 3 tablespoons of the sausage fat from the pan and add the chopped onion. Brown the onion in the fat, stir in the flour and cook for a minute or so. Stir in the broth and cook the gravy for about 5 minutes to thicken. Return the sausage cakes to the skillet and heat thoroughly in the gravy.

Serves 4 to 6

"Frying the Fastnachts"

Fastnachts were made only once a year – on Fastnacht Day (Shrove Tuesday) or the night before.

Sponge:

Usually at night milk was scalded and cooled. The yeast was dissolved in warm water and added to the milk. Sugar and flour were added to the mixture and set in a warm place to allow to raise overnight.

Dough:

In the morning, more sugar, melted butter, salt, eggs and flour were added to the sponge and mixed well. It was allowed to raise again until light. Then the dough was rolled out on a well-floured board, and cut into squares, triangles, rectangles, or even 5-sided cuts, and slits were cut into each one. They were then covered to prevent drying out and let to raise again. They were then fried in hot fat on the wood or coal stove until brown.

To eat, the fastnachts were cut in half horizontally, and spread with molasses, quince honey, crabapple jelly, honey or apple butter. Or they were dusted with powdered sugar or a cinnamon and sugar mixture.

They were served with coffee or dunked in blue balsam or saffron tea.

–*Gladys Lutz*

FASTNACHTS

4 cups sugar
6 eggs
2 tsp. salt
3 cups raw potatoes, diced
1 cup butter
1 cup shortening
milk
2 pkg. yeast
6-7 lbs. flour

Mix the sugar, eggs and salt. Cover the potatoes with enough water to cover them by about one inch and cook until tender. Drain the potatoes, reserving water, and mash without adding anything. Melt the butter and shortening. Add milk to the potato water to make four cups. Do not cool anything. Add mashed potatoes, milk mixture and melted butter to the egg mixture. Mix thoroughly. Sprinkle the yeast over this mixture and mix again. Gradually add the flour until dough is stiff and can be worked. Knead until smooth and let rise in a warm place until it is doubled, about 3-4 hours. Roll out about one inch thick and cut into shapes. Lay each shape on a cloth covered table, cover and let rise again. Fry in 385 degree hot fat, turning once, until brown. Drain on paper towels and cool. Makes 100 fastnachts.

MOLASSES CRUMB CAKE

Frances Wright Trexler

This is great served warm with a late Sunday morning breakfast of scrambled eggs and bacon.

1/3 cup butter
2 cups flour
1 cup sugar
1 tsp. each nutmeg, cloves and cinnamon

Mix thoroughly and set aside 1 cup of the dry mixture. To remaining crumbs add:

1 egg
1 tsp. baking soda
2 Tbsp. unsulphered molasses
1 cup sour milk

Pour batter into two greased cake pans. Divide crumbs evenly between both cakes and bake at 350 degrees for 20-25 minutes or until toothpick come out clean.

MARY WRIGHT'S ONE-RISE CINNAMON ROLLS

This is the only cinnamon roll recipe you will ever need. Try them Christmas morning.

TOPPING
1 cup heavy cream
1 cup brown sugar

FILLING
1/2 cup white sugar
2 tsp. cinnamon
1/3 cup softened butter

ROLLS
3-3 1/2 cups flour
1 pkg. dry yeast
1/4 cup sugar
1 tsp. salt
1 cup hot tap water
2 Tbsp. butter
1 egg

For the Topping: combine the cream and brown sugar and mix well. Do not whip. Place in the bottom of an ungreased 9x13 glass pan. Add one cup chopped nuts or raisins if you wish.

For the Filling: Mix together sugar, cinnamon and butter and set aside.

For the Rolls: Mix 1 1/2 cups flour with the remaining roll ingredients. Beat well and add remaining flour. Knead one minute. Press or roll dough into a 15x7 inch rectangle. Spread the filling over the dough. Starting with the long side, roll up and cut into 16-20 rolls. Place on top of topping in pan. Cover and place in a warm place to rise until doubled, 35-45 minutes. Bake at 400 degrees for 20-25 minutes. Turn our on a foil lined tray. Allow enough foil to catch any syrup.

This dough can be made the day before and refrigerated overnight. In the morning place a towel over the pan of rolls and microwave on warm or 10% power for ten minutes, allow to sit in microwave for 20 minutes and bake as directed.

"Cutting Out the Christmas Cookies"

In the days of wood stoves, Christmas cookie baking started weeks before the holiday in the Dutch country. The tin cookie cutters in the form of every animal in Noah's ark were washed because they had not been used since the year before.

Many kinds were baked but the animal cookies or apees were the favorite. Cookies were baked by the lard can full or the wash basket full. Why? The family consumed many cookies, some were displayed in the front windows for passers-by to see, some were hung on the Christmas tree, some were eaten by the Belsnickels and some were given to the poor widows living near by. Many were big cookies, perhaps 6 or 8 inches across the middle for dunking. Our thin wafer-like cookies of today would not have been liked then.

In general, the recipe calls for 1 lb. of butter, 2 cups of sugar, 4 eggs well beaten. Then add 6 cups flour and 1 rounded tsp. soda. Mix well and chill the dough overnight.

When ready to bake, dust the baking board well with flour, roll out a small portion of dough and using the cookie cutter, cut out the shapes. Place on cookie tins and and decorate with green or red sugar, hickory nuts or other nuts. Bake in a moderately heated oven for 7 to 10 minutes.

To this day, apees cookies and the other cookies are still made by families who hold fast to tradition. However, everything is made in a quicker and more modern way.

–Gladys Lutz

COCONUT GINGEROONS

1 stick butter
1/2 cup brown sugar
1/4 cup unsulphered molasses
1 egg
1/2 tsp. baking powder
1 1/2 tsp. ground ginger
1/2 tsp. cinnamon
1/2 tsp. ground coriander
1/2 tsp. salt
1 cup shredded coconut
sugar for rolling

Cream butter, brown sugar and molasses. Add the egg. Sift dry ingredients together and add to creamed mixture. Chill dough several hours. Line cookie sheets with aluminum foil or parchment (cookies will stick and burn without this). Roll cookies into one inch balls and dip one end in water and then in sugar. Place on cookie sheets and press down slightly. Bake in a 375 degree oven for 12-15 minutes. Store in an airtight container.

MIRIAM YODER'S COCONUT COOKIES

1 cup sugar
1 cup butter
1 egg
1 tsp. vanilla
1 tsp. cream of tartar
1/2 tsp. baking soda dissolved in a little hot water or vinegar
1 cup coconut
2 cups flour

Cream butter and sugar. Add the egg, vanilla, baking soda, flour and coconut. Form into logs and chill. Slice and bake at 375 degrees for 8-10 minutes or until the edges are brown.

MOLASSES ROLLOUT COOKIES

1 cup unsulphered molasses
1 cup brown sugar
1 cup butter
1 Tbsp. baking soda
5-6 cups flour
1/2 tsp. salt
1/2 tsp. nutmeg
1 tsp. ground ginger
1 tsp. cinnamon
1 egg, well beaten

Combine molasses, sugar, butter and baking soda in a heavy saucepan. Bring to a boil, stirring constantly and boil slowly for five minutes. Cool thoroughly. Mix and sift salt, spices and flour. Add egg to the molasses mixture and then thoroughly combine with the dry ingredients. Chill. Roll 1/4 inch thick and cut with your favorite cookie cutters. Bake at 375 for 8-10 minutes. Can be iced with Icing for Sarah's Sugar Cookies.

Variation: Add 1 1/2 cups shredded coconut to the flour before adding molasses. Chill and roll into balls to bake.

MORAVIAN SAND TARTS

This is a very delicate cookie that lends itself well to any special occasion.

2 cups butter
2 1/2 cups confectioners sugar
5 eggs
4 cups flour
1 tsp. baking powder

Cream butter, sugar and eggs. Add baking powder and flour. Dough will be rather soft. Divide into four balls and refrigerate overnight. Remove one ball of dough from refrigerator at a time. It works best when it is well chilled. Roll out thinly on a floured cloth or board. Cut out with simple cookie cutters. These cookies are best done as circles, hearts or other geometric shapes. Transfer to cookie sheet and brush with one beaten egg mixed with a few tsps. of water. Dust with cinnamon sugar and place a small nut meat of any kind in the center. Bake at 350 degrees until edges just begin to brown, 8-10 minutes. Watch them carefully as they will burn quickly. Remove to cooling rack and handle carefully.

SARAH OBYLE'S SUGAR COOKIES

2/3 cup margarine
1 1/3 cup sugar
2 eggs
1/2 tsp. vanilla
1/3 cup milk
2/3 tsp. baking soda
4 cups flour

Cream margarine and sugar until well blended. Add eggs, vanilla, milk and baking soda. Gradually add flour. Roll out and cut with your favorite cookie cutters. Bake at 350 degrees 10-12 minutes or until edges brown lightly.

ICING FOR SARAH'S SUGAR COOKIES

3/4 lb. confectioner's sugar
1/2 stick butter
1 tsp. vanilla
milk to moisten

Cream butter and add sugar and vanilla. May be colored with food dye. Ice cookies and let dry before storing in air tight tin.

SUGAR AND SPICE COOKIES

3/4 cup soft butter
1 cup sugar
1 egg
1/4 cup unsulphered molasses
2 cups flour
2 tsp. baking soda
1/4 tsp. salt
1 tsp. each cinnamon, cloves and ginger

Cream butter and sugar, add egg and molasses. Mix in dry ingredients.

Form into one inch balls and place two inches apart on greased cookie sheet.

Bake 10-12 minutes at 350 degrees. When baked and slightly set but still warm, roll in sifted confectioner's sugar.

THREE GINGER COOKIES

¾ cup butter at room temperature
1 cup brown sugar
¼ cup unsulphered molasses
1 egg
2¼ cups flour
2 tsp. ground ginger
2 tsp. baking soda
½ tsp. salt
1½ Tbsp. finely chopped ginger root
½ cup finely chopped crystallized candied ginger

Cream butter and sugar. Add egg and molasses. Mix in soda, salt and gingers.

Add flour. Refrigerate dough overnight or until firm. Roll into one inch balls and place two inches apart on greased cookie sheets. Bake 10-12 minutes at 350 degrees.

HOT CHOCOLATE VOLCANOES

A chewy chocolate cookie with a secret ingredient.

1½ sticks butter
⅔ cup unsweetened cocoa
¾ cup granulated sugar
¾ cup brown sugar
¼ tsp. hot red cayenne pepper
¾ tsp. salt
1½ tsp. baking soda
2 eggs
2 cups flour
½ cup chocolate chips

Heat the butter in a large saucepan until melted. Remove from heat and whisk in cocoa, sugars, cayenne and salt until smooth. Stir in the eggs.

Sift the flour and baking soda into the pan and stir until blended completely. Add the chocolate chips. Form dough into a ball and chill until firm. Roll the dough into one inch balls, roll in granulated sugar, place on an ungreased cookie sheet and bake at 375 degrees for 10-12 minutes or until the tops are cracked. Do not overbake the cookies or they will lose their chewiness. Store in an airtight container.

ARGO MOLASSES COOKIES

1 cup butter
1/2 cup shortening
2 cups sugar
1/2 cup unsulphered molasses
2 large eggs
4 tsp. baking soda
2 tsp. each cinnamon, ginger and cloves
1 tsp. salt
4 cups flour

Preheat oven to 375 degrees. Cream butter, shortening, sugar and molasses. Add eggs. Sift together dry ingredients and add to creamed mixture. Mix until a stiff dough is formed. Form into 1 inch balls and roll in granulated sugar. Place on an ungreased cookie sheet and bake for 12 minutes or until crackled but somewhat soft. Store in an airtight can. These cookies keep well for several weeks.

CHOCOLATE NUT WAFERS

This is a thin tasty cookie appropriate for Christmas or any occasion. The recipe can be doubled.

1/2 cup butter
1 cup sugar
1 egg
1 tsp. vanilla
2 squares unsweetened chocolate
    (melted according to package directions)
3/4 cup sifted flour
3/4 tsp. salt
3/4 cup finely chopped walnuts

Cream butter and sugar. Add egg and vanilla. Stir in the melted chocolate and add flour, salt and walnuts. Drop from a teaspoon onto a lightly greased cookie sheet and press down with the bottom of a smooth glass that has been dipped in water. Bake 10-12 minutes at 325 degrees.

Winter

EVELYN DUNKELBERGER'S MOLASSES COCONUT PIE

2 Tbsp. flour
1/2 tsp. baking soda
1 cup granulated sugar
2 eggs, beaten
1 cup table molasses or (1/2 cup table molasses and 1/2 cup unsulphered molasses)
1 cup milk
1/2 cup sweet or sour cream
1 cup coconut

Mix the flour, baking soda and sugar. Add the beaten eggs and mix well. Add molasses, milk, cream and coconut. Bake in an 8 or 9-inch piecrust at 375 degrees for 50 minutes.

RAISIN PIE

This pie was commonly served at the gathering of friends that occurs when a loved one dies. Consequently, you may also find recipes like this titled "Funeral Pie".

1 cup seedless golden raisins
2 cups of hot water
1 egg
1 cup sugar
2 Tbsp. cornstarch
Pinch salt
1/4 tsp. nutmeg
Juice and rind of 1 lemon
1 Tbsp. butter

Soak the raisins in the hot water until they are soft and plump. This may take an hour or more. Do this in a medium saucepan.

Preheat the oven to 375 degrees.

Thoroughly whisk the rest of the ingredients together and stir into the raisins. Cook over moderately low heat until the filling thickens. Cool slightly and pour the filling into a well-chilled piecrust. Bake in the lower third of the oven for 10 minutes then reduce the heat to 350 and continue baking 20 minutes more.

This is great with pie crumb topping. If you choose to include them, sprinkle them over the filling before baking.

PUMPKIN NUT ROLL

1 cup sugar
3 eggs
2/3 cup pumpkin
3/4 cup flour
1 tsp. baking soda
2 tsp. cinnamon
1 cup walnuts or pecans, chopped

Beat eggs in an electric mixer for five minutes. Add sugar, pumpkin, flour, baking soda and cinnamon. Mix well. Grease a 15x10x1/2 inch cookie sheet. Line the sheet with waxed paper and grease the wax paper. Pour the batter in the pan and sprinkle with nuts.

Bake at 375 degrees for fifteen minutes. Meanwhile place two paper towels on a tray and dust with powdered sugar. When the pumpkin roll is done, turn it upside down on the paper towels and roll up the cake in the towels. Chill the pumpkin roll completely before unrolling and filling with Cream Cheese Filling. Chill until firm and slice to serve. This freezes very well and makes a great gift at Christmas time.

CREAM CHEESE FILLING

1 cup powdered sugar
8 ounces cream cheese
1/2 tsp. vanilla
4 Tbsp. butter

Cream butter and cream cheese, add the sugar and vanilla and mix well.

CHOCOLATE BREAD PUDDING

2 cups whole milk
2 cups whipping cream
1 cup sugar
8 ounces semisweet chocolate, chopped
8 large eggs
1 Tbsp. vanilla extract
4 cups cubed white bread or egg bread, crusts trimmed

Preheat the oven to 350°F. Combine the milk, cream and sugar in a heavy large saucepan over medium-high heat. Stir until sugar dissolves and mixture comes to a boil. Remove from heat. Add the chocolate and stir until smooth. Beat the eggs and vanilla in large bowl to blend. Gradually whisk in the chocolate mixture. Add the bread cubes and let stand until the bread absorbs some of custard, stirring occasionally, about 30 minutes.

Transfer the mixture to a 13x9x2-inch buttered glass baking dish. Cover with foil. Bake until set in the center, about 45 minutes. Uncover and cool at least 15 minutes before serving.

Serve warm or at room temperature with whipped cream or caramel sauce or both.

Serves 12

Winter

HELLO DOLLIES

A fittingly sweet ending to our collection of recipes, these were made for me by Gladys Lutz on one of my trips to her home to purchase the paintings that are reproduced in this book. –J.D.

- 1 stick melted butter
- 1 1/2 cup graham cracker crumbs (12 whole crackers)
- 1 14 oz. can sweetened condensed milk
- 6 oz. chocolate chips
- 1 1/3 cups coconut
- 1 cup chopped walnuts

Combine the melted butter and the graham cracker crumbs and press into the bottom of a 9 x 13 baking pan. Pour the condensed milk over the crumbs. Sprinkle the remaining ingredients evenly over the crumbs and press down lightly. Bake in a 350-degree oven for 30 minutes. Cool and cut into small squares. As this is quite rich, a small piece goes a long way.

Index

Breads, Biscuits and Coffee Cakes
Baking Powder Biscuits 10
Chocolate Bread Pudding 92
Cinnamon Rhubarb Muffins 20
Fastnachts. 82
Gary's Bread. 28
Mary Wright's One-Rise Cinnamon Rolls 83
Molasses Crumb Cake. 82
Oatmeal Bread 28
Potato Bread 29

Cakes and Frostings
Apple Butter Cake. 62
Angel Food Cake. 43
Chocolate Fudge Frosting 44
Coconut Sour Cream Cake 23
Gingerbread 66
Hickory Nut Cake 66
Karen's Chocolate Cake 43
Mrs. Elwood's Cake 42
Peanut Butter Frosting 44
Pumpkin Nut Roll 92
Rhubarb Cake 20
Rhubarb Pecan Upside Down Cake 18
Spice Cake 67

Cookies, Candy and Ice Cream
Argo Molasses Cookies. 90
Black Raspberry Sauce 45
Chocolate Nut Wafers 90
Coconut Candy. 23
Coconut Gingeroons 86
Folk Festival Vanilla Ice Cream 44
Hello Dollies 93
Hot Chocolate Volcanoes 89
Miriam Yoder's Coconut Cookies 86
Molasses Roll Out Cookies 87
Moravian Sand Tarts. 87
Peach Ice Cream 45
Potato Candy 23
Rhubarb Bars 21
Sarah Oblye's Sugar Cookies. 88
Sugar and Spice Cookies 88
Three Ginger Cookies 89
Vernette Meyer's Vanilla Ice Cream. 45

Eggs and Fritters
Breakfast Casserole. 55
Corn Fritters 30
Deviled Eggs 33
Double Boiler Scrambled Eggs 11

Kris Amey's Peach Fritters 39
Oyster Corn Fritters 30
Pickled Red Beet Eggs 14

Meats and Main Dishes
Baked Sauerkraut and Pork Chops 75
Corn Pie 29
Creamed Chicken 10
Creamed Dried Beef 72
Dotty Brett's Chicken Potpie 54
Ham and Beans in a Crockpot 51
Ham and String Beans 72
Marinated Roast Venison Tenderloin 73
Oven Fried Chicken 35
Potato Onion Pie 61
Pig Stomach 74
Pork and Sauerkraut 73
Pork Tenderloin with Rhubarb and
   Dried Currant Chutney 11
Sausage with Gravy 79
Simple Pot Roast 79
Venison Tenderloin with Apple Butter Marinade 55

Pastries and Pies
Apple Crisp 62
Apple Pie 61
Basic Pie Crumbs 22
Basic Pie Crust 22
Buttermilk Custard 22
Corn Pie 29
Egg Custard Pie 39
Elsie Snyder's Lemon Strip Pie 63
Evelyn Dunkelberger's Molasses Coconut Pie 91
Harriet's Rhubarb Pie 19
Lemon Sponge Pie 63
Mae Bittner's Shoofly Pie 38
Potato Onion Pie 61
Pumpkin Pie 62
Raisin Pie 91
Rhubarb Crisp 19
Rhubarb Custard Pie 15
Rhubarb Torte 21
Simple Rhubarb Custard Pie 18
Shoofly Pie 38
Sour Cherry Pie 42

Preserves and Relishes

Beet Relish 58
Best Tomato Catsup 31
Bread and Butter Pickles 32
Cranberry Orange Relish 58
Gloria Hamm's Black Raspberry Jam 31
Grated Horseradish 12
Strawberry Jam 31

Salads and Dressings

Creamy Dandelion Dressing 13
Cucumber Salad 30
Dutch Cole Slaw 33
Green Bean Salad 59
Hot Bacon Dressing 13
Pepper Cabbage 58
Jane Dietrich's Potato Salad 34
Red Pepper and Cucumber Salad 30
Summer Potato Salad 32

Soups

Chicken Corn Noodle Soup 50
Oyster Stew 74
Potato Corn Chowder 50
Roasted Squash Soup 51

Vegetables and Side Dishes

Baked Asparagus with Lemon Sauce 12
Barley Casserole 61
Basic Mashed Potatoes 75
Braised Red Cabbage 60
Corn Bread Stuffing 55
Creamed Spinach 11
Creamy Scalloped Potatoes 75
Fried Tomatoes with Milk Gravy 35
Green Beans with Tomatoes 60
Harvard Beets 12
Pan Browned Brussel Sprouts 59
Potato Filling 78
Raw Potato Pancakes 78
Rhubarb Applesauce 18
Roasted Asparagus 12
Scalloped Tomatoes 34
Stewed Rhubarb 15